Individual Accounts for Social Security Reform

Individual Accounts for Social Security Reform

International Perspectives on the U.S. Debate

John Turner

2006

W.E. Upjohn Institute for Employment Research
Kalamazoo, Michigan

Library of Congress Cataloging-in-Publication Data

Turner, John A. (John Andrew), 1949 July 9-
    Individual accounts for social security reform : international perspectives on the U.S. debate / John Turner.
        p. cm.
    Includes bibliographical references and index.
    ISBN-13: 978-0-88099-282-4 (pbk. : alk. paper)
    ISBN-10: 0-88099-282-4 (pbk : alk. paper)
    ISBN-13: 978-0-88099-283-1 (hardcover : alk. paper)
    ISBN-10: 0-88099-283-2 (hardcover : alk. paper)
    1. Social security—United States. 2. Social security individual investment accounts—United States. I. Title.
    HD7125.T847 2005
    348.4'300973—dc22

2005028378

© 2006
W.E. Upjohn Institute for Employment Research
300 S. Westnedge Avenue
Kalamazoo, Michigan 49007-4686

Cover design by Alcorn Publication Design.
Index prepared by Diane Worden.
Printed in the United States of America.

Contents

Boxes

Tables

Acknowledgments

I began thinking about this book while working in Geneva, Switzerland, for the International Labor Office on a volume on social security reform around the world (*Social Security Pensions: Development and Reform* [Gillion et al. 2000]). This current book follows the structure of an Upjohn Institute volume I coauthored while on a Fulbright at the Institut de Recherches Economique et Sociale in Paris, *Private Pension Policies in Industrialized Countries: A Comparative Analysis* (Turner and Watanabe 1995), which focuses primarily on voluntarily provided defined benefit plans. The pension world has changed considerably since that time, and defined contribution plans are playing an increasingly dominant role.

Besides having drawn on my work for those two books, I have greatly benefited from collaboration over many years with distinguished coauthors, whose work with me I have cited, and to whom I express gratitude: Clive Bailey, Daniel Beller, David Blake, Richard Burkhauser, Yung-Ping Chen, Lorna Dailey, Philip DeJong, William Even, Colin Gillion, Roy Guenther, Richard Hinz, Sophie Korczyk, Denis Latulippe, David McCarthy, David Rajnes, Patricia Reagan, Martin Rein, and Noriyasu Watanabe. I have received helpful comments from three anonymous reviewers; from Susan Friedman, the book's primary editor; from Alan Gustman; Karen Holden; Estella James; David McCarthy; Pamela Perun; Anne Stewart; and Kevin Hollenbeck. Joanne Brodsky and Sophie Korczyk read the entire book and made numerous valuable comments. It should be noted that several reviewers generously provided comments in spite of not agreeing with some aspects of the book. I must thank Claire Black, Erika Jackson, and Ben Jones of the Upjohn Institute for typesetting and editing the numerous changes to the manuscript. I also wish to thank my wife, Kathy, and daughter, Sarah, for supporting my absences to write, attend conferences, and work abroad. And I wish to thank my parents, Henry and Mary, for ultimately making everything possible.

In addition, I would like to express appreciation to AARP for permitting me to write this book. The work on this project was not done during my hours of employ by AARP. The opinions expressed here are entirely my own responsibility and do not necessarily represent the policy positions of AARP.

1
Individual Accounts and Social Security Reform

Defined contribution pension plans providing workers with individual accounts dominate pension plan growth worldwide. Contributions are made into the accounts, usually by workers and sometimes by employers. The return on the investment of the funds is credited to the account. The participating worker usually has some choice over the investment of the account and bears the resulting financial risk. At retirement, the participant can convert the account balance to an annuity, receive it as a lump sum, or take benefits through phased withdrawals, depending on the rules governing the plan.

As recently as the early 1980s, defined contribution plans were an unimportant source of retirement income. In contrast, defined benefit plans have traditionally been the plan chosen by most countries for social security and by most employers who provide pensions for their employees. Such plans provide benefits determined by a formula that usually takes into account the worker's earnings and years of service. The risk associated with the financing that underlies defined benefit plans is not borne by the worker but by the plan sponsor or an insurance company. While there has been impressive growth in the number of countries that have adopted mandatory defined contribution plans, social security programs worldwide are still dominated by defined benefit plans.

As the popularity of mandatory defined contribution plans has spread, the names by which such plans are called have multiplied. Those names, which have political significance, differ in focus as to what element of the plan is stressed; some examples include personal retirement accounts, retirement savings accounts, private accounts, and individual accounts. This book follows the terminology used in publications of the National Academy of Social Insurance and refers to them as individual accounts.

Countries have adopted mandatory individual accounts primarily in Latin America and in Central and Eastern Europe, where the predecessor social security plans faced serious financial problems, but Hong

Kong, Sweden, and the United Kingdom are other notable examples. Twelve Latin American nations have adopted them, accounting for roughly half the population of Latin America, although only about half the labor force of these countries is covered (Gill, Packard, and Yermo 2005). Voluntary defined contribution plans have grown in importance in many high-income countries of the Organisation for Economic Co-operation and Development (OECD), particularly in the English-speaking countries of Australia, Canada, Ireland, the United Kingdom, and the United States. In the United States, 401(k) plans—an employer-provided individual account plan typically requiring employee contributions—have grown rapidly and are now the most common type of pension plan (USDOL 2005).

The structure of the book is as follows: after this general introduction, the second chapter introduces the topic of individual accounts, discusses the framework used to analyze them, and looks at the key issue of risk. The third chapter surveys the main issues in the social security reform debate and looks at social security reform involving individual accounts, as well as the use of individual accounts in social security systems around the world. The fourth and fifth chapters treat issues in the financial management of individual accounts: the fourth chapter looks at those issues that arise when agents (the officers of corporations and the managers of mutual funds) manage investments; the fifth chapter discusses problems that individuals encounter as a result of their own investment decisions. Chapter 6 examines labor market issues arising from individual accounts. Specifically, it looks at these accounts' effects on workers' behavior and on income distribution. The seventh chapter discusses the forms in which individual accounts pay benefits and the taxation of individual accounts. Chapter 8 provides a summary of the book.

Appendices A and B provide information relevant to the U.S. Social Security reform debate but treat topics that are of less general interest than those covered in the chapters. They present more technical subjects and are offered for readers who may have a more detailed interest in these areas. Rate-of-return guarantees, discussed in Appendix A, have been included in some proposals but have not been an aspect of the proposals associated with the Bush administration. Contribution evasion, discussed in Appendix B, has not been an issue in the reform debate, but it may be an important issue for self-employed workers and workers who are paid in cash.

IT BEGINS WITH A POLITICAL DECISION

Including individual accounts in social security is a political decision. However, that choice results from the interplay of a country's underlying cultural, economic, and demographic forces, as well as the financial status of its social security plan. As influenced by a country's culture, retirement income systems reflect differing political philosophies concerning individualism versus collective social responsibility and the roles of government, employers, the financial sector, families, individuals, and private charity.

In countries where social solidarity and communal responsibility for the less fortunate are important values, government plays a major role in retirement income through traditional defined benefit plans that provide social insurance. In countries placing a high value on individual responsibility and free choice, the private sector's role is larger, either through voluntary employer-provided plans or through individual accounts that are part of the social security system. Some countries favor individual accounts as a way of widening the range of personal choice and increasing reliance on the private sector. Even those countries, however, maintain a large mandatory element in their social security programs by requiring participation.

Ideology is a component of the political culture, but economic and demographic factors also affect the structure of retirement income systems. In upper-income countries, the development of domestic capital markets, containing the skilled personnel and the regulatory structure required to ensure their efficient functioning, plays a part in determining the possible role of individual accounts. In the United States, the development of 401(k) plans, providing workers with a familiarity with the functioning of individual accounts, has doubtlessly paved the way for the increased acceptability among American voters of individual accounts as a part of Social Security, although the replacement of defined benefit plans with 401(k) plans as the dominant plan type has also raised the level of financial risk borne by American workers.[1]

Population aging is a fundamental demographic force affecting retirement income systems. It occurs both through increased life expectancy and through reduced birth rates. It raises the ratio of retirees to workers, reducing social security's internal rate of return that workers receive as determined by the relationship between contributions and benefits for pay-as-you-go social security programs. "Pay as you go" means that the program has enough money to provide current benefits but that it does not have a reserve for future benefits. Population aging, by raising the old-age dependency ratio (the ratio of retirees to workers), favors the development of funded pensions, which can be either defined benefit or defined contribution. Funded pensions have a reserve for paying future benefits.

Although population aging is often cited as a reason for switching from a traditional social security plan to a defined contribution individual account, defined contribution plans are not immune to the effects of demographic change. Increased life expectancy at retirement age raises the number of years in retirement and thus the costs of providing a given level of annual benefits in both defined benefit and defined contribution systems.

SOCIAL SECURITY REFORM WITH
INDIVIDUAL ACCOUNTS

Should social security benefits be provided through individual accounts? The answer depends in part on whether those plans are add-ons to social security or carve-outs that reduce the value of social security benefits. This book considers public policy issues concerning individual accounts as part of a national social security system. It analyzes policies several countries have adopted. International experience provides insights as to the range of policy options and the effects of different approaches.

This book has several themes. First, the desirability of individual accounts in social security reform depends on their role in retirement income and whether they reduce or supplement social security. Thus, the plans cannot be judged in isolation, but must be evaluated according to their role in the retirement income system.

Second, while individual accounts as part of social security can be designed so that they are simple and benign, having little or no effect on the behavior of workers, generally they are complicated in their structure and effects. The complexity of individual accounts is often not appreciated in policy debates, in part because of the comparatively short history of experience with them in social security systems. Policy analysts, for example, generally have treated them as not affecting the behavior of workers, believing that they are similar to voluntary savings plans. Because the actual details of plan structure are important, this book provides descriptive detail about the operations of the major types of mandatory individual accounts.

Third, risk in individual accounts occurs in many different forms, not solely because of the financial market. This topic is raised in various sections of the book. From most perspectives, individual accounts are riskier than are defined benefit plans in high-income countries that have well-managed social security systems. The aspects of risk affect the role of individual accounts in providing retirement income.

This book relies primarily on economic analysis and foreign experience for assessing mandatory individual accounts, but it also discusses 401(k) plans and the Thrift Savings Plan for federal government workers. The focus is on issues relevant to including individual accounts in social security in the United States and in other high-income countries.

International comparisons of individual accounts may be particularly useful for U.S. policymakers. While the U.S. experience is limited to voluntary plans, a number of countries have experience with individual accounts that are part of social security. The relevance for the United States of the policy experience in other countries is assessed, taking into consideration, for example, additional sources of retirement income that may affect the structure and functioning of individual accounts. International experience, when properly applied, can provide insights for the United States into both the successes and the failures of other countries' policies. In some cases, the lessons from policy failures are that the problems are fixable; in other cases, the failures indicate problems inherent in the particular structure of an individual account system.

THE BIG PICTURE: THE ROLES OF TRADITIONAL SOCIAL SECURITY PLANS AND INDIVIDUAL ACCOUNTS

Much of this book focuses on the microeconomics of how mandatory individual accounts function. The big picture, by contrast, concerns how these plans fit into a retirement income system (World Bank 1994; Gillion et al. 2000). To conclude this chapter, I will comment on issues affecting the big picture.

Most recent reforms of social security have been driven in part by the need to restore solvency to traditional systems in the face of population aging. In this context, add-on individual accounts generally have no effect on solvency because their financing is independent of that of the traditional social security program. Carve-out individual accounts generally worsen solvency issues over a transition period lasting decades because of the need to continue financing the benefits in the traditional social security program. Thus, in social security reform debates, it is important to separate the issues of individual accounts and social security solvency.

Some analysts have focused on social insurance issues and the prevention of old-age poverty (Gill, Packard, and Yermo 2005). Within this framework, the roles of different types of pension plans are compared, based on their ability to provide insurance by transferring income across people and to shift income from the individual's working period to retirement. One view is that the need for social insurance is diminishing as the risk of old-age poverty declines. The contention is that the function of mandatory savings for retirement should occur through individual accounts, but that poverty prevention should occur though mandatory defined benefit plans.

Other analysts, however, have focused on the ability of different types of pension plans to spur national savings and economic growth (World Bank 1994). They argue that mandatory individual accounts should be used to encourage savings and growth. In this context, it is important to distinguish between carve-out and add-on accounts. Carve-out accounts are less likely to add to national savings, in part because they replace benefits that were already provided and in part because they reduce the financing for the traditional social security program.

Another perspective places relatively more emphasis on risk-bearing by workers and the risks of different types of pension plans (Gillion et al. 2000). Analysis indicates that in countries where policy risk is relatively small, mandatory individual accounts generally are considerably more risky than are traditional social security plans.

THE GOAL OF THE BOOK

The primary goal of this book is to provide a better understanding of how individual accounts would work if they were adopted in the United States as part of Social Security reform. It is important when new approaches are being considered to carefully think about how they might work, evaluating both their positive and their negative aspects. That is done by using the tools of economics and learning from the experiences of other countries. The next chapter will acquaint the reader with different types of defined contribution plans and the financial structure and management of individual accounts. It will also detail the many risks inherent in mandatory individual accounts.

Note

1. The term "social security" is capitalized when referring to the U.S. Old Age and Survivors Insurance (OASI) program. The term "workers" is generally taken to include the self-employed in the U.S. context.

2
Introduction to Individual Accounts

TYPES OF DEFINED CONTRIBUTION PLANS

This book starts out with some basics. The first two sections of this chapter consider different types of defined contribution plans and take a broader perspective than most of the remainder of the book. Although the focus of the book narrows in subsequent chapters, the following types of defined contribution plans are discussed in this book.

Voluntary Defined Contribution Plans

These exist in Ireland, Canada, and the United States and are prevalent in about a dozen other countries. Employers provide the plans voluntarily in order to attract the caliber of employee they wish to hire.

Mandatory Individual Accounts

Argentina, Chile, Peru, Mexico, Poland, Sweden, and Hong Kong have these plans (Gillion et al. 2000). The large majority of countries around the world, however, provide social security old-age benefits through a mandatory defined benefit system, based on principles of social insurance. Most high-income countries have such programs, but an increasing number of countries provide social security benefits through mandatory defined contribution programs.

Mandatory Employer-Provided Defined Contribution Plans

These are found in Switzerland, Australia, and Denmark (Rein and Turner 2001). Such plans have become the foundation for a mandatory system in some of the high-income countries of the OECD, where widespread employer-sponsored pensions have existed for many years on a voluntary basis. These mandated plans can be either defined benefit or defined contribution; in Switzerland, a hybrid combining both defined benefit and defined contribution features is commonly used (Turner and Rajnes 2003).

Widespread Collective Bargaining

Sweden, Denmark, and the Netherlands have quasi mandating of employer-provided plans, but this is not a statutory requirement. Rather, it derives from a legal framework that supports collective bargaining and from the resulting contractual agreements between labor unions and employers that cover most workers in the country.

Voluntary Carve-Out Individual Accounts (VCOs)

In the United Kingdom, these plans allow workers to voluntarily substitute an alternative for part of social security. Called "contracting out" in the United Kingdom, this type refers to a system where workers or firms, depending on the arrangements, can voluntarily withdraw from part of social security if they provide a replacement pension plan at least as generous. (See Box 2.1, Voluntary Carve-Out Accounts around the World.)

Provident Funds

A number of former British colonies, such as Singapore, have these government-managed individual accounts. Provident funds are national mandatory savings plans that generally pay benefits in a single payment, a lump sum benefit. While other types of social security programs offer survivors and disability benefits and provide benefits as an annuity, provident funds usually only provide a lump sum retirement benefit. Malaysia and Indonesia have large provident funds. A number of countries in Africa and the Caribbean have terminated their provident fund plans in favor of traditional defined benefit plans that provide social insurance.

The contribution rate in different types of plans varies considerably based on the role of the plan for the retirement income system. Table 2.1 shows the contribution rate for some individual account plans in different countries. While contribution rates for traditional defined benefit social security programs have risen in a number of countries, the rates for mandatory individual account plans have been stable.

Box 2.1 Voluntary Carve-Out Accounts around the World

Voluntary carve-out accounts (VCOs) are often a transitional feature of mandatory pension systems, being offered to workers above a certain age as a way of "grandfathering" them into a program that is being modified for new participants. They are less commonly an ongoing feature available to new workers entering the labor force. The United Kingdom, however, has such a system of "contracting out" of the state pension scheme as an ongoing aspect of its retirement income system.[a] VCOs were proposed in the United States in 1935 in the Clark amendment to the original Social Security Act; they were rejected because voluntary participation was viewed as inconsistent with the redistributive nature of the U.S. Social Security system (Schieber and Shoven 1999). Defined benefit VCOs are used in Japan and the United Kingdom; however, among the high-income countries of the OECD, only the United Kingdom allows VCOs to be defined contribution individual account plans.

VCOs are also used by Colombia and Peru in their individual accounts systems (Gillion et al. 2000). VCOs are a feature of the provident funds in India, Sri Lanka, Nepal, Fiji, and Gambia. Malaysia allows VCOs for teachers, the military, the self-employed, and domestic workers. In Greece, workers with approved pension plans providing at least equivalent benefits are allowed out of the entire public system.

[a] It goes by the name of the State Second Pension (S2P) Scheme. Before April 2002 it was called the State Earnings-Related Pension Scheme (SERPS).

THE FINANCIAL STRUCTURE OF INDIVIDUAL ACCOUNTS

The preceding section described types of defined contribution plans but did not present a structure for how they relate to each other. This section highlights important differences among types of defined contri-

Table 2.1 Contribution Rates in Individual Account Plans in Selected Countries, 2005

Type of plan	Country	Name of plan	Contribution rate (%)
Mandatory, funded	Australia	Superannuation Guarantee charge	9.0
	Chile	Administradoras de Fondos de Pensiones	10.0
	Denmark	ATP	Flat amount
	Mexico	Administradoras de Fondos de Retiro	6.5
	Sweden	Premium Pension	2.5
	Switzerland	BVG/LPP	7.0–8.0, increasing with age
Contracted-out, funded	United Kingdom	Approved Personal Pension	4.6
Mandatory, unfunded	France	ARRCO (employees)	14.0 min.
		AGIRC (managers)	14.0 min.
	Italy	Notional account	33.0
	Sweden	Notional account	16.5
Voluntary, group	Canada	Registered Pension Plan	18.0 max.
	United Kingdom	Personal Pensions	17.5 max.
	United States	401(k), profit sharing, money purchase	18.0 max.
Voluntary, individual	Canada	Registered Retirement Savings Plan	18.0 max.
	United States	Individual Retirement Account	$4,000 ($4,500 if age 50+)

NOTE: There are generally minimum and maximum limitations on the earnings to which the contribution rates apply. Maximum contribution rates in voluntary plans may be lower if the worker contributes to another plan. The maximum contribution rate in the United Kingdom for Personal Pensions is higher for workers aged 40 and older. Some countries have two tiers within their social security system, or have both voluntary and mandatory plans, and thus are listed twice in the table.

SOURCE: Gillion et al. (2000); ISSA (2003).

bution plans by looking at the incentives that motivate their provision and their relationship to social security plans.

Four Pathways to Pension Coverage: Degrees of Compulsion

Countries have developed a dizzying variety of policies to encourage the development of both defined contribution and defined benefit plans. The resulting plans, however, can be grouped into four pathways to pension coverage; these are differentiated by the degree of incentive or compulsion provided to workers to participate in the plan (Rein and Turner 2001). In terms of degree of compulsion, these four categories include 1) unrestrained choice for the worker (including whether to participate in a pension plan), 2) a compulsory arrangement determined by collective bargaining between employers and trade unions, 3) a choice between two alternatives—participating in a pension provided either by the government or by the private sector—and 4) a government-imposed mandate. Often a country uses multiple pathways to encourage pension coverage and participation.

1) Voluntary participation, with tax incentives

The pathway the United States uses to encourage employers to provide pension coverage, both defined contribution and defined benefit, is voluntary with tax incentives. Employers are not required to provide pensions, and employees are not required to be covered. The only compulsion is that regulations stipulate that an employer who voluntarily offers a plan must cover, or offer coverage to, most or all workers.

A strength of this policy is that it maintains free choice for workers and employers. However, practically without exception, no more than half the workforce is covered in countries that use this approach (Dailey and Turner 1992). With this approach, coverage rates tend to be relatively low among low-wage workers (Hinz and Turner 1998).

A variant of this approach is automatic enrollment with an opt-out: individuals are automatically enrolled in a plan but have the option of opting out. Another variant is to require that employers offer a plan but not require that the employee participate. These two options maintain the voluntary approach but with added degrees of compulsion. These approaches are alternatives to outright mandates.

2) Collective bargaining

A second pathway to expanding pension coverage, and one with an element of mandating, is widespread collective bargaining. In some countries where all or most of the labor force is covered by a collective bargaining agreement, a high percentage of workers have pension coverage through plans resulting from collective bargaining. Countries using this approach include France, the Netherlands, Denmark, Norway, and Sweden. This strategy can only be used when a large portion of the labor force is covered by a union or where, as in the Netherlands, under law a collective bargaining agreement can be mandatorily extended to other firms in the same line of business. This approach is thus not feasible for the United States, with its low level of union membership.

3) Voluntary carve-outs

The remaining two pathways to pension coverage, voluntary carve-outs and mandatory individual accounts, are the focus of this book. The voluntary carve-out approach involves requiring participation in a retirement income plan but permits a choice between participating in social security or in an alternative private plan. With voluntary carve-outs, the employer and the worker may reduce or end their contribution to social security if the worker participates in a private sector plan that provides benefits meeting at least minimum requirements. For workers who choose the voluntary carve-out, the smaller contribution to social security lowers the benefit the worker ultimately receives from that source, but the worker receives an added benefit through the individual account. An advantage of voluntary carve-outs is that they maintain free choice, and they may encourage private sector provision of pension plans.

In Japan, voluntary carve-outs have been provided on a fairly neutral basis with respect to the incentive for participation—the government has neither subsidized nor disfavored participation. The United Kingdom, in the past, has encouraged voluntary carve-outs by providing them on a subsidized basis. Voluntary carve-out accounts were proposed for the United States by President George W. Bush in his second inaugural address and his subsequent State of the Union message.

The voluntary nature of this approach may create the problem of adverse selection. With adverse selection, the workers who most benefit from taking a voluntary carve-out leave the social security system, eroding its financial base. For example, in the United States, depending on the way voluntary carve-outs would be structured, and on the extent to which the Social Security system redistributes income from upper-income to lower-income workers, individuals with higher incomes may be more likely to take a voluntary carve-out than those with lower incomes. For these reasons, some observers view full mandating as preferable.

4) Mandating

Mandating individual accounts is an alternative to mandatorily raising retirement income benefits by increasing the Social Security payroll tax and benefit level. While Social Security provides a uniform structure of benefits and contributions across the workforce, mandatory individual accounts generally allow greater flexibility and diversity in the types of arrangements. The mandatory approach can either compel employers to provide a pension plan for their workers or require workers to have an individual account plan with a third-party provider.

Australia and Switzerland mandate employer provision of pensions. In Sweden, the government collects the pension contributions and distributes them to the mutual funds chosen by workers, with the employer's only role being to transmit the workers' contributions to the government. Mandatory pension systems that supplement a traditional social security program often do not cover all workers; they may exclude low-wage, part-time, and short-tenure workers.

Relationship to Social Security

An alternative approach to understanding the different types of individual accounts is to classify them according to their relationship to social security. Pensions can either be add-ons to or carve-outs from social security. An add-on is a pension plan that supplements the social security benefit. The social security benefit is unaffected by the provision of the add-on. A carve-out, by comparison, replaces part or all of the social security benefit (Box 2.2). In reforms that completely replace an old system with a new one (such as in Sweden), this distinction can get blurred. However, it is a major distinction in reforms such as the type being considered in the United States.

Box 2.2 The Difference between Add-On and Carve-Out Accounts

An add-on account is an individual account that is added to an existing social security program. A carve-out account is an individual account that replaces benefits in an existing social security program. While these distinctions are clear when individual accounts are combined with social security programs that already exist, the distinctions can be fuzzy when a new social security program is enacted.

In the United Kingdom, an earnings-related social security program was not established until the 1970s. At that time, there were already well-established employer-provided defined benefit plans. Contracting out (voluntary carve-outs) was permitted to protect the existing employer-provided pensions rather than reduce the benefits in an already existing social security program.

In Sweden in 1999, an existing defined benefit social security program was replaced with a smaller program (receiving lower contributions) and new mandatory individual accounts. From the U.S. perspective, the Swedish individual account system can be considered to be an add-on because it comes on top of a generous base program supported by a payroll tax of 16 percent. Further, it does not reduce the benefits of a preexisting program since it was created at a time when a new social security program was being established. However, from the Swedish perspective, it might be considered a mandatory carve-out in that it reduces the level of contributions going to the defined-benefit social security program, relative to the old program that was replaced.

Add-ons and carve-outs can be either voluntary or mandatory. This taxonomy results in four categories of pension plans: voluntary add-ons, mandatory add-ons, voluntary carve-outs, and mandatory carve-outs. This book focuses on three of these four types of defined contribution pensions: mandatory add-ons, voluntary carve-outs, and mandatory carve-outs. Table 2.2 provides examples of countries in these categories.

Table 2.2 A Simple Categorization of Types of Individual Accounts, Selected Countries

Relationship	Degree of compulsion	
to social security	Voluntary	Mandatory
Add-on	Canada, United States	France, Switzerland
Carve-out	Japan, United Kingdom, Colombia, Peru	Chile, Mexico, Uruguay

SOURCE: Rein and Turner (2004).

Full or Partial Replacement of Social Security

A further dimension of carve-outs is the extent to which they replace social security. Carve-outs can either partially or completely supplant the existing social security system.

The role of defined contribution pensions within the retirement income system is often expressed by the imagery of tiers of programs. The World Bank (1994) has favored a three-level approach in which the first tier is a basic government-provided benefit program designed to alleviate poverty; the second tier is a mandatory, funded, privatized program; and the third tier is a voluntary, funded program. The number of tiers in this framework can be increased by recognizing the role of an antipoverty benefit, informal intergenerational transfers, private savings, and work in old age.

The World Bank framework recognizes the important distinction between a partial replacement of social security in a three-tier system and the full replacement of social security in a single-tier or two-tier approach. With this expanded framework, individual accounts can be incorporated in a social security system in five ways: 1) voluntary carve-outs that partially replace social security (for example, in the United Kingdom), 2) voluntary carve-outs that fully replace social security (Colombia), 3) mandatory carve-outs that partially replace social security (Uruguay), 4) mandatory carve-outs that fully replace social security (Chile), and 5) mandatory add-ons to social security (Sweden). Table 2.3 provides examples of countries in the different categories of individual accounts.

The approaches that are most relevant for the debate in the United States are voluntary carve-outs that partially replace social security and

Table 2.3 An Expanded Categorization of Types of Individual Accounts

Relationship to social security	Degree of compulsion		
	Voluntary	Widespread contractual agreements	Mandatory
Add-on	Canada, United States	Netherlands, Sweden	Sweden
Partial carve-out	United Kingdom		Uruguay
Full replacement	Colombia, Peru		Chile, Mexico

NOTE: Blank = not applicable.
SOURCE: Author's compilation.

mandatory add-ons. For that reason, much of this book focuses on the experience of the United Kingdom and Sweden when drawing on foreign experience. Chile is also often viewed as a model for social security reform. Although its particular form of full replacement of social security is not being seriously considered in the United States, there are lessons to be learned from aspects of its experience. Table 2.4 provides an overview of the individual accounts in these three countries.

In comparing the retirement income systems for various countries, it is important to keep in mind key economic and demographic differences. Table 2.5 compares the United States with Chile, Sweden, and the United Kingdom. Chile and Sweden have considerably less than one-tenth the population of the United States (the United Kingdom's population is also much smaller—about one-fifth that of the United States), and Chile has much lower per capita income. The poverty rate in Sweden is markedly below that in the United States. Such factors affect the operation of the retirement income systems of these countries.

FINANCIAL MANAGEMENT OF INDIVIDUAL ACCOUNTS

Another dimension of the structure of individual accounts is their financial management. Both add-on and carve-out accounts can be managed at least three ways: 1) the Chilean model of individual accounts managed by pension fund companies, 2) the Australian model

Table 2.4 Overview of Mandatory Individual Accounts in Chile, Sweden, and the United Kingdom

	Chile	Country Sweden	United Kingdom
Type of DC system[a]	Mandatory full replacement of social security	Small add-on to social security	Voluntary carve-out from social security
Role in retirement income system	Major	Supplemental	Shared role
Contribution rate for mandatory DC plan[a]	10%	2.5%	Variable, depending on age
Centralized management	No—management by individual pension funds	Yes—government clearinghouse	No—government clearinghouse for contributions, but individual accounts held with service providers
Individual choice	Choice of pension fund manager, each manager offers 5 different funds	Choice of up to 5 funds from over 600 mutual funds	Choice of insurance company or other service provider
Rate-of-return guarantee for investments	Guarantee relative to return received by other plans	No	No
Rate-of-return guarantee for annuity conversion	No	Yes, a minimum of 3%	No
Mandatory annuitization	No	Yes	Yes, at age 75
Cost-of-living indexation of benefits	Yes	No	Yes
Mandatory survivors benefits	Yes, for women	No	No
Redistribution toward lower-income workers	No	No	No

[a] DC = defined contribution.

SOURCE: Author's compilation.

Table 2.5 Economic and Demographic Statistics for the United States, Chile, Sweden, and the United Kingdom, 2004

	Country			
Characteristics	United States	Chile	Sweden	United Kingdom
Population (millions)	293	16	9	60
Population 65+ (%)	12.4	7.8	17.3	15.7
Life expectancy at birth (yrs.)	77.4	76.4	80.3	78.3
GDP per capita[a] (000s $)	37.8	9.9	26.8	27.7
Population below poverty line (%)	12	21	1	17

[a] Gross domestic product per capita.
SOURCE: CIA (2005).

of mandatory employer-provided pensions, and 3) the Swedish model of individual accounts managed by a government clearinghouse. With the Chilean model, the accounts are managed in a decentralized fashion by private sector pension fund management companies. In Chile, individual workers choose a pension fund management company and direct their employer to send their contribution to that company each month. With the Australian model, accounts are managed by individual employers, and each employer establishes a plan for company employees.

In Sweden, the government plays a major role in the management of individual accounts. The government serves as a clearinghouse to which employers send their workers' contributions. The government also acts as a record keeper and disburses the appropriate amounts to each of the pension funds in which a worker has elected to invest.

This book does not consider mandates that require employers to provide pensions, based on the political judgment that that approach is the least likely to be chosen by the United States, and instead focuses on the Chilean and Swedish models for pension fund management. Thus, the Australian approach is not considered, though some lessons are drawn from aspects of its experience.

The Chilean model involves decentralized management by pension funds, while the Swedish model involves centralized management by a government clearinghouse. The Swedish model has the advantage of having lower administrative costs than the Chilean model, but it involves a larger role for the government, illustrating the trade-off between these factors. Many people favoring individual accounts do so in part because they believe this policy will lead to a reduced role for the government in the provision of retirement income. With individual accounts, there may be a reduced government role in the sense that payroll taxes are reduced, but at the same time the government bureaucracy may grow because of the role of the government clearinghouse.

ELEVEN RISKS IN MANDATORY INDIVIDUAL ACCOUNTS

The risks in individual accounts should be viewed in the context of all sources of retirement income a worker expects to receive. The risks are greater if the individual accounts replace a stable base of social security benefits than if the individual accounts are an add-on to social security. It may be optimal for most workers to diversify and bear the risks both of the traditional social security program and of financial market assets, though that does not necessarily imply a mandated individual account system.

While financial market risks are clearly an issue with individual accounts, there are numerous other kinds of contingencies that are less frequently considered. Many of the concerns regarding risks in individual accounts do not even arise in defined benefit plans. This section introduces the types of risk that affect pension participants in individual accounts. The topic is dealt with in greater detail subsequently in the book.

Individual accounts can be invested in government bonds and constructed with various guarantees, and thus some of the risks they commonly entail are not necessarily inherent. Adding guarantees, however, imposes a cost that lowers the expected rate of return.

Risks while Working

Investment risk

In individual accounts, financial market risk has traditionally been borne entirely by the worker, while in employer-provided defined benefit plans it is primarily borne by the employer or by an insurance company. The increasing role of individual accounts, both as voluntary and as mandatory plans, raises the importance of the financial risk-bearing by workers and retirees. Some analysts argue that individual accounts, when they are the primary source of retirement income, place too much financial market risk on workers (Ferguson and Blackwell 1995). When these accounts play a minor role, however, being provided on top of a secure, low-risk base of traditional social security and a defined benefit employer-provided pension plan, the concerns are less serious.

Especially for low-income workers who rely to a large extent on social security benefits for retirement, it is important that this source provide stable benefits, at least for a substantial part of retirement income. Workers generally are risk-averse, and some—women, low-income workers, and those with limited education—are especially so (Hinz, McCarthy, and Turner 1996). Others, however, argue that the greater financial risk the worker assumes with individual accounts is more than offset by increased expected benefit levels (Feldstein, Ranguelova, and Samwick 1999).

Investment risk arises in financial markets because of the changes in the real (inflation-adjusted) value of assets and their rates of return. The risk of a stock market bubble may result from "irrational exuberance" by investors. The potential for loss can be reduced at the expense of expected rates of return by investing in more secure assets such as government bonds, by purchasing an insurance company product, or by establishing rate-of-return guarantees (discussed in Appendix A).

If a person were to maintain a constant portfolio mix over his or her career, the possibility of a large loss would increase as the worker came closer to retirement because the account balance would be larger. Workers can offset this risk by gradually moving into bonds, but because of inertia it appears that many do not make that change (Turner 2003).

By contrast, as workers approach retirement age, the risk of a large loss in social security decreases. This occurs for two reasons. First, in the United States, Social Security benefits are based on an individual's career average earnings, and most of those amounts would already be known as a worker got closer to retirement. Second, most reform proposals are designed so that they do not affect workers aged 55 and older; thus, the chance of legislative changes altering benefits is considerably less for older workers than for younger workers.

Agency risk

In addition to financial market risk on stock investments arising from swings in the macroeconomy, individual account participants are also subject to losses from improper financial management of their investments. Agency risk occurs because the pension participant's investments are handled by agents rather than directly by the individual. The agents include mutual funds and the corporations whose shares the pension participant holds. This risk is borne by the plan sponsor in funded defined benefit plans but by the worker in individual accounts.

Individual management risk

Individual management risk arises from individual errors in managing pension investments. Evidence has accumulated that many individuals systematically make errors in managing pension investments, and that these errors affect their retirement income (Turner 2003). An example of individual management risk is the tendency of some people to buy a stock or mutual fund after its price has risen and to sell it after its price has fallen, resulting in a buy-high-and-sell-low pattern. Individual management risk does not occur in traditional defined benefit social security plans but does arise in individual account plans.

Policy risk

Policy risk results from changes in national tax and retirement income policy that affect the level of benefits received from a pension. Such changes can affect participants in both defined benefit plans and individual accounts. In the voluntary carve-out plans in the United Kingdom, every five years the Government Actuary's Department (GAD) resets the key parameter determining the generosity of the benefits received from social security and from the carve-out individual account. Public policy risk is greater in many countries for young participants in traditional social security programs than for those in individual accounts. As previously discussed, financial risk is typically higher than policy risk for workers near retirement.

Risk of adverse labor market outcomes

The unemployment risk to retirement income stems from the worker experiencing periods of joblessness. Unemployment and being out of the labor force have less of an impact on benefits in the U.S. Social Security program than they do in an individual account plan because benefits are based on a person's 35 highest years of earnings. At least for many individuals who have full careers of work, a period of unemployment may have no effect on their Social Security retirement benefits but would affect benefits in an individual account plan.

Retirement benefits are influenced more by unemployment when workers are young than when they are old because of the impact of interest compounding. Related to this, being out of the labor force for any reason has a bigger effect on retirement benefits for workers in an individual account when they are young than when they are old. For example, young women who take off time to rear children may greatly reduce their retirement benefits in an individual account plan.

Related to unemployment risk is the possibility of receiving lower pay than expected. This could be due to changes in the fortunes of the employer or industry where one works, or it could be because of personal issues such as poor health. Defined benefit social security plans provide insurance against these situations since their benefit formula is designed to provide redistribution to lower-earning workers.

Risk of disability

The risk of becoming disabled before retirement and unable to work is not dealt with by individual accounts. Workers who become disabled at a young age only have the amount that has accumulated in their accounts. This contingency must be dealt with outside individual accounts through the purchase of disability insurance.

Risk of premature death

The risk of premature death is that of dying young and leaving behind juvenile dependents (Nyce and Schieber 2005). Defined contribution plans deal poorly with this possibility because a worker who dies young likely would not have accumulated sufficient assets to provide for children. A defined benefit social security program can cover this by including survivor benefits for young workers, which provide better protection. With individual accounts, this situation must be handled separately through the purchase of survivors insurance.

Risks at and in Retirement

Replacement rate risk

Replacement rate risk involves the possibility that workers will have a lower income replacement rate than expected. The income replacement rate is the percentage of preretirement earnings provided by retirement income and is affected by the risks associated with both the financial market and the worker's preretirement earnings. In defined benefit plans the worker bears part of this risk (the part arising because of uncertain wages), and in individual accounts the worker completely bears the risk.

Annuitization (interest rate) risk

An annuity is a stream of benefits received for life. Individuals may be required in an individual account system to convert their account balances into an annuity by using the account balance to purchase an annuity from a life insurance company. Annuitization risk arises because of changes in interest rates and reflects the possibility that the individual annuitizes his or her account balance when interest rates are down, resulting in low annual benefits. Annuitization risk does not arise in defined benefit social security plans because they delineate the benefit level irrespective of the level of interest rates.

Longevity risk

Longevity risk for workers occurs both before and during retirement, and it has both a cohort and an individual component. First, there is the element related to changing cohort mortality rates up to the point of retirement. This situation affects the annuity value if the individual decides to annuitize the account balance, or the amount the person can take out through phased withdrawals if not choosing to annuitize. Second, longevity risk after retirement for people who annuitize their individual accounts is borne by the annuity provider, typically an insurance company. Alternatively, individuals who do not annuitize their account balances face the prospect of living longer than expected and not having sufficient funds. Both aspects of longevity risk are borne by the plan sponsor in defined benefit plans providing annuitized benefits.

Inflation risk

Inflation risk arises from price level increases that occur after retirement. Generally, capital market assets keep pace with inflation, so that concern is not an important issue before retirement for reasonable levels of inflation. However, if benefits are not price-indexed, inflation after retirement will erode their real value. Traditional defined benefit social security plans usually provide full price-indexing, while that typically is not provided in individual accounts, although Chile and the United Kingdom are exceptions.

Risks Affecting Pay-as-You-Go Social Security

There are also risks that affect pay-as-you-go defined benefit plans but do not affect individual accounts and funded defined benefit plans. One example is dependency rate risk, which reflects shifts in population age structure that occur because of changes in rates of birth and mortality. The old-age dependency ratio can be measured as the ratio of retirees to workers. It acts as a shadow price for social security benefits (Turner 1984). If there is one retiree for every four workers, it costs each worker $0.25 to raise the benefit level of the retirees by $1. If the old-age dependency ratio doubles and there is one retiree for every two workers, it costs each worker $0.50 to raise the benefit level of retirees by $1. Pay-as-you-go defined benefit plans are subject to the risk of changes in the old-age dependency ratio, while individual accounts are not.

In sum, when considering different ways of providing social security benefits, in nearly all respects individual accounts are riskier than a well-managed defined benefit social security plan such as is found in the United States. This is true for risks related to the issues of individual management investments, adverse labor market outcomes, disability, premature death, earnings replacement, annuitization, longevity, and inflation. Traditional social security plans are riskier for older workers with respect to changes in the old-age dependency rule, and for younger workers with respect to changes in public policy.

CONCLUSIONS

Individual accounts can be categorized either with respect to the incentive for their provision or with respect to their relationship to social security pensions. Combining these two approaches, social security reform using individual accounts can occur in five different ways: 1) voluntary carve-outs that partially replace social security (United Kingdom), 2) voluntary carve-outs that fully replace social security (Colombia), 3) mandatory add-ons to social security (Sweden), 4) mandatory carve-outs that partially replace social security (Uruguay), and 5) mandatory carve-outs that fully replace social security (Chile). Of these approaches, this book, in the context of possible U.S. reforms, focuses on three: voluntary carve-outs that partially replace social security, mandatory add-ons, and mandatory carve-outs that partially replace social security. The effects of individual accounts depend on which type of account is being considered. It is important to distinguish between add-ons and carve-outs.

Another dimension of the structure of individual accounts is their financial management. For either add-on or carve-out accounts, individual accounts can be managed in at least three ways: by using the Chilean model, the Australian model, or the Swedish model. This book focuses on the Chilean and Swedish models of financial management as being the approaches most relevant for the United States to consider. When considering overall approaches, the book focuses on Sweden and the United Kingdom as leading examples of the add-on and carve-out approaches.

3

Individual Accounts in Social Security Reform: The Debate

A high-stakes debate is raging among politicians, policy analysts, and concerned citizens over the use of individual accounts for Social Security reform in the United States. Some participants are partisans with strongly held positions that are rooted in fundamental differences in political philosophy. Some politicians and other commentators have used the words "looming" and "crisis."

Mandating individual accounts appeals to some people on both economic and ideological grounds. From the economic standpoint, they argue that mandatory individual accounts would increase savings and reduce government's role in the economy. From the ideological perspective, they contend that those pensions would enhance individual freedom, private property ownership, and personal responsibility, while reducing government's role in the economy (President's Commission 2001).

Others, however, argue that individual accounts that fully or partially replace a traditional defined benefit social security system may entail too much financial market risk, especially for vulnerable retirees (Gillion et al. 2000). Individual accounts that are carve-outs would generate high transition costs over a period of decades to pay benefits already promised in the old system. Individual accounts that are add-ons to social security, however, may be viewed differently because they retain social security as the traditional base of retirement income. They do not involve transition costs because they do not reduce funds allocated to pay for social security benefits already promised.

THE PROS AND CONS

Why Some Countries Use Individual Accounts for Social Security

Some policy analysts and international financial institutions, including the World Bank, have advanced a number of reasons for using individual accounts for social security (World Bank 1994). These arguments differ between plans that reduce an existing social security program and those that are an add-on to such a program.

Those who argue for individual accounts as part of social security reform, whether as mandatory add-ons or as voluntary carve-outs, generally believe such accounts would result in the following economic advantages:

- Improved functioning of capital markets
- Increased national savings
- Higher real (inflation-adjusted) rates of return
- Improved functioning of labor markets
- Reduced overall level of risk for workers

These issues are discussed in turn.

Improved functioning of capital markets

Some observers have credited individual accounts with encouraging the development of national stock markets and increasing national savings in countries in which financial markets were poorly developed before their introduction (Piñera 2001). Such effects on financial institutions are less likely to occur in the United States, which already has an established capital market.

Increased national savings

One of the most complex aspects of the debate is how individual accounts would affect savings. Individual accounts may increase national savings by substituting a funded account for an unfunded one; however, critics argue that the accounts could instead substitute for savings that would otherwise occur, especially among higher-income workers, many of whom already have substantial savings (Gale and Scholz

1994). Substitution for other forms of savings would be less likely to occur among lower-income workers because of their lower probability of having savings. To the extent that substitution occurs, any positive effect on savings is diminished.

Substitution could also occur through workers' taking on additional debt to offset the added savings. Workers could do so to avoid the reduction in consumption that would occur if savings were to increase. For example, homeowners could increase their mortgage debt by refinancing their homes. The additional debt could offset the increase in financial market assets held in individual accounts.

Substitution that would offset increased savings would be especially likely with voluntary carve-out individual accounts, as opposed to mandatory accounts; this would occur because the workers likely to choose them have higher incomes and would already have savings in taxed accounts outside pension plans. They could switch their taxed savings into a tax-preferred individual account and, because of the tax advantage, would need to save less to reach a given target amount.

Further, some argue that boosting national saving can be accomplished through other means and should not be considered a function of social security. For example, an alternative would be to reduce the federal deficit by raising non–social security taxes and cutting non–social security spending (Cutler 1999).

Analysts opposed to mandatory individual accounts also have argued that, for the same reasons that social security is compulsory (i.e., because many people would not save sufficiently on their own), people will want to have access to their individual accounts before retirement. That also would reduce any positive effect on savings. The experience with Individual Retirement Accounts (IRAs) may be instructive. Because of political pressure, the law has been relaxed over the years since the inception of IRAs in 1974, allowing easier access to these accounts before retirement.

The effect of individual accounts on national savings also depends on other changes that are made in the government budget. If the government were to finance the transition to individual accounts with increased government borrowing, that would offset whatever increase in savings might occur among workers, in terms of net savings in the economy. The transition cost is the cost of paying for benefits that have already been promised but for which additional financing would be needed if privatizing reduces the financing of the existing social security system. This transition cost can be large, and the transition period can last for five decades or longer. In Chile, for example, the transition cost peaked at nearly 5 percent of Gross Domestic Product (GDP) during the first decade of the reform, and even after 40 years the transition cost is projected to be more than 1 percent of GDP (Edwards 1998).

In the United States, Social Security has temporarily accumulated a large trust fund. With voluntary carve-out accounts, the amount in the trust fund would be reduced, as money paid out in benefits would not be replaced by payroll taxes. Some economists have argued from a national perspective that the increase in the trust fund has been offset by non–Social Security deficits. This shift in government financing from income taxes to payroll taxes may have increased savings to the extent that income taxpayers have a higher marginal propensity to save than payroll taxpayers (Diamond and Orszag 2004).

As is the case in other countries, a fundamental issue concerns whether encouraging national savings should be a primary responsibility of Social Security. Some commentators have argued that government tax and budgetary policy should assume that role (Gillion et al. 2000).

In sum, although the issues regarding social security and savings are unresolved, a shift to individual accounts, particularly voluntary carve-out accounts, may not increase national savings. In any case, there are other aspects of national economic policy that affect savings; thus, encouraging savings need not be a requirement of social security reform, especially if the proposed reforms reduce the insurance protections provided by social security.

High real rates of return

Some supporters of mandating individual accounts have projected high real rates of return, and indeed that has been the case in Chile. For each of the seven Chilean pension fund management companies (Administradoras de Fondos de Pensiones, or AFPs) in 2002, the real rate of return over the period 1982–2002 averaged at least 10 percent. Although these returns are high, they represent gross rates of return not subtracting fees and expenses. Once fees and expenses are taken into account, the cumulative average real rate of return is 6.8 percent for low-income workers and 7.1 percent for high-income workers.

However, even these adjusted figures overstate the rates of return received by workers because they are simple average rates of return, while the geometric average is the appropriate measure (Williamson 2005). The geometric average provides the rate of return that if earned continuously over the period would produce the actual ending balance. A Chilean brokerage firm used data for the years 1982–1998 and calculated an average real geometric rate of return net of expenses of 5.1 percent. By comparison, if the worker had instead purchased Chilean 90-day bank deposits each month, the average compound rate of return would have been 7.2 percent (CB Capitales 1999; Williamson 2005).

Individual account holders in other countries have not fared as well; the systems in Sweden, Hungary, and Poland, for example, experienced negative real rates of return for their first few years of operation because of the downturn in world capital markets during the early 2000s. These results highlight the fact that systems should not be judged based on rates of return experienced over a short period, which are subject to random fluctuations. An extended time period is more relevant for judging a long-term investment such as social security. Nonetheless, short-term fluctuations in capital markets can be a major risk for individual account participants who are nearing retirement.

In the United States, debate has arisen over the appropriate rate of return to credit individual accounts when prospectively comparing them with Social Security. Some correction should be made for the greater financial risk inherent in individual accounts that are invested in equities, with the extreme argument being that the rate of return credited should be that on bonds because the higher return on equities is due to the risk premium on equities. In any case, comparisons of rates of return between social security and individual accounts need to make some adjustment for risk.

Improved functioning of labor markets

Some policy analysts have thought that converting to individual accounts would reduce contribution evasion—the failure of workers and employers to make required payments—because benefits would be tied more closely to payments (World Bank 1994). Contribution evasion, however, remains a problem in many of the Latin American countries, especially among lower-paid or temporary workers and among employees in the informal sector (Bailey and Turner 2001). The informal sector consists of casual employment that evades government regulation and taxation. Contribution evasion for social security occurs even in highly developed countries such as the United States, mainly in the underground economy and among self-employed workers. (See Appendix B for further discussion of contribution evasion.)

Reduced level of retirement income risk

Some argue that the use of individual accounts would reduce the overall level of risk that workers face concerning their retirement income (President's Commission 2001). The choice between government or private provision of retirement income is affected by an assessment of the risks associated with each method, including the risks of financial markets compared with the political risks of having underfunded social security programs.

Why Some People Oppose Individual Accounts for Social Security Reform

It is important to distinguish between add-on and carve-out individual accounts. The opposition to individual accounts by some people concerns their use as carve-out accounts. Some policy analysts and international financial institutions, such as the International Labor Organization (Gillion et al. 2000), have argued against using carve-out individual accounts. Perhaps the chief rationale against mandating carve-out accounts is that they place too great a burden of financial risk on low-income workers, especially when the plans replace part of a traditional social security program, reducing the base level of benefits. With mandatory individual accounts that are an add-on to social security, the argument concerning financial market risk is weakened.

With mandatory individual accounts, the worker has an asset that is invested in the capital market and bears the risk of financial market fluctuations. When the worker reaches retirement, he or she generally also bears the risk of fluctuations in interest rates in determining the annuity value of the account balance. Workers differ in their attitudes toward financial market risk and in their knowledge about these markets. Typically, low-income workers are more risk-averse and less informed than higher-income workers concerning the investment of their retirement income.

A response to this criticism concerning risk-bearing in carve-out individual accounts is that workers may have the option of investing their accounts in low-risk assets. Further, it has been argued that risks would be reduced by diversifying sources of retirement income instead of relying exclusively on a pay-as-you-go system. Underfunded social security systems are also subject to the risk that workers will not receive all of the benefits promised or that contribution rates will be raised, although those risks are generally considerably smaller for older workers than capital market risks, in part because benefit cuts and tax increases impose political costs on policymakers.

A further issue is the extent to which guarantees are incorporated within the system (see Appendix A at the end of the book). Many countries with mandated individual accounts incorporate rate-of-return guarantees (for example, Argentina and Chile), but a sizable number, including Australia and Sweden, do not (Turner and Rajnes 2001). Such guarantees mitigate the adverse effects of market fluctuations on account holders.

Issues Arising from Mandatory Individual Accounts

Private sector management of individual account investments is generally viewed as the most important aspect of the substitution of a private role for a government role in the provision of social security. Financial management, however, is only one of several retirement income functions that can be privatized. Other functions include record keeping for the accounts of beneficiaries, the choice of fund managers, collection of contributions and disbursement to fund managers, annuitization of benefits, disbursement of nonannuitized benefits, and the insurance or provision of guarantees for promised benefits. All privatized social security systems maintain government involvement in some of these functions, which sometimes is extensive (Turner and Rajnes 1998).

In developing social security systems with individual accounts, countries must consider the extent to which worker choice is allowed. Generally, the greater the range of choice, the greater the system's administrative cost because of the added complexity in administering the program. Will workers be allowed to choose from few investment funds or many? Will they be allowed to transfer money across funds at any time or once a quarter? How many funds will they be allowed to hold at one time? These are some of the typical questions countries adopting such a system must resolve.

VOLUNTARY CARVE-OUT ACCOUNTS

The issues arising from incorporating individual accounts into social security depend on the type of accounts used. Although the literature on individual accounts is extensive, of the basic types of individual accounts, the least attention has been paid to voluntary carve-out accounts (exceptions include Blake 1995; Turner and Rajnes 1995; Gustman and Steinmeier 1998; Kotlikoff, Smetters, and Walliser 1998; Disney, Palacios, and Whitehouse 1999; Orszag and Greenstein 2001; and NASI 2005). Yet voluntary carve-outs can be the most complex type of individual account. (See Box 3.1 for some of the problems the United Kingdom encountered with voluntary carve-out accounts.)

With a voluntary carve-out, the worker has a choice. He or she can remain in the social security system or withdraw from it, either partially or fully, depending on the structure of the voluntary carve-out. In exchange for a reduction in both current taxes and future social security benefits, the worker is obliged to contribute to an individual account. The employer's contributions to social security may also be transferred to the individual account.

In the mid-1990s, the United States considered a carve-out health insurance reform based on "pay or play" (Turner and Rajnes 1995). Voluntary carve-outs for social security had been proposed in the United States in 1935 as the Clark Amendment to the original Social Security Act; however, these were rejected by Congress because voluntary participation was thought to be inconsistent with the redistributive nature of the U.S. Social Security system (Schieber and Shoven 1999).

The genesis of voluntary carve-outs in the United Kingdom came from completely different reasons from those motivating President Bush's proposal as put forth in his 2000 and 2004 presidential campaigns. The United Kingdom was quite late in establishing an earnings-related social security program; this was not done until the 1970s. At that time, a well-established private pension sector was already in place.

Box 3.1 Problems Encountered with Voluntary Carve-Out Accounts in the United Kingdom

Since 1988, the United Kingdom has allowed employees to voluntarily withdraw from part of social security by reducing their contributions and receiving lower benefits. Instead, employees contribute to an individual account. In 2005, a pension commission in the United Kingdom proposed abolishing this system (Pensions Commission 2005). This system of voluntary carve-out accounts (VCOs) has resulted in various problems.

Workers Are Being Encouraged to Leave the Individual Account System

Insurance companies are encouraging many policyholders to stop contributing to their VCOs and to return to the traditional social security program. The British government determines the benefit offset, the amount by which social security benefits are reduced for workers who choose the VCO. Although not its intent, the government set the VCO benefit offset so that it is no longer favorable for most workers to take the VCO, according to some British insurance companies. Every five years, the British government determines the amounts that are credited to individual accounts for workers taking a VCO. In 2002, interest rates were low, but the British government expected that they would rise. Thus they credited individual accounts at a lower level, assuming workers would be able to earn higher rates of return on their accounts. When interest rates did not rise, the amount workers were earning on their investments in their VCO accounts was insufficient to compensate them for the reduction in their social security benefits. Two large insurance companies, Prudential and Norwich Union, sent letters to their 750,000 policyholders with VCOs telling them that they would be better off leaving their VCOs and returning to the traditional social security program (Money Marketing 2004). In 2004, 500,000 people abandoned VCO pensions and returned to the state system (Cohen 2005).

The Government Paid Large Subsidies to Participants in the Individual Accounts

VCOs resulted in a large government subsidy in the early years. The British government initially established a favorable benefit offset for

Box 3.1 (continued)

workers to encourage them to choose VCOs. It subsequently estimated that the present value of the savings due to the reduction in future benefits was $22 billion less than the cost to the government in incentives provided to take a VCO. The cost to the government in incentives to take a VCO was roughly twice as much as it saved through reduced benefit payments (Budd and Campbell 1998).

Individual Accounts Have Been a Bad Deal for Many Workers

A number of people are financially worse off for having taken the VCO. Because of many workers' lack of financial sophistication, pension service providers who have a financial interest in workers' choosing accounts, even when those accounts are inappropriate for the individual, may have taken advantage of VCO participants. In the United Kingdom, with the "pensions mis-selling" scandal, more than two million people contributed to VCO accounts who would have been better off remaining in social security. Those affected represent more than 40 percent of workers who initially took VCOs with personal pensions, and the compensation they will receive from financial service providers as a result of being misled is approximately $20 billion. The people mis-sold were primarily lower-wage workers (Gillion et al. 2000).

There Is a Long Lag between the Collection and Crediting of Contributions to the VCOs

The government does not credit contributions to VCOs until 18 months after the start of the tax year in which the worker made the contributions, and it pays no interest during this period. While a system could be established to credit accounts more quickly, such a system would increase administrative costs because it would require more record keeping.

VCOs Have High Administrative Costs

In 1998, the combined effect of the fees charged on VCO accounts equaled an average reduction in yield of 3.2 percent per year for people who had participated in these plans for 10 years and a projected rate of 1.7 percent per year for people who would stay for 25 years (Blake and Board 2000).

Voluntary carve-outs were permitted in the United Kingdom not to reduce a preexisting social security program but to protect a preexisting defined benefit private pension system. Later, for ideological reasons relating to the encouragement of individual responsibility by Margaret Thatcher's Tory government, workers were allowed to establish private accounts to reduce their participation in social security.

Generosity of the Trade-Off

The trade-off between contributions to an individual account and reductions in future social security benefits is probably the most important aspect of the structure of voluntary carve-outs, and it is the most difficult feature to structure to avoid distortions in the retirement income system.

The smaller the reduction in the worker's future social security benefits that accompanies the reduction in the worker's social security payroll taxes, the more favorable to the worker is the voluntary carve-out, and the more likely it is to be chosen. However, another directly related trade-off exists: the more favorable the voluntary carve-out is to the worker, the more costly it is to the government. A generous voluntary carve-out may result in a substantial subsidy of individual accounts by the traditional social security system or by government general revenue (Box 3.2).

The problem of setting the trade-off's generosity is highlighted by the report of the President's Commission (2001), which in its three proposals set three different rates. It proposes reducing future social security benefits the worker will receive by an amount based on the decrease in payroll taxes that is compounded by a real interest rate ranging from 2.0 to 3.5 percent.[1] President George W. Bush suggested a real rate of 3.0 percent (above inflation) during his second term.

The benefit offset determines the voluntary carve-out's effect on social security's long-run solvency. If workers are required to forgo a portion of benefits actuarially equivalent to what would have been paid for by the reduction in their social security payroll taxes, social security's finances will not be affected over the long run. A transition effect occurs, however, because social security contributions are decreased years before benefit payments are reduced. If the benefit offset deviates from actuarial equivalence, it will affect the desirability to workers of taking

---

Box 3.2   Voluntary Carve-Outs in Japan

In Japan, voluntary carve-outs from social security can be done only by using employer-provided defined benefit plans. Nonetheless, aspects of the Japanese experience are relevant for assessing voluntary carve-outs that use individual accounts. In any type of carve-out system, it is difficult to calibrate the requirements for the carve-out plan. In Japan, many employers have decided that they are unable to obtain the financial rate of return necessary to provide the benefits required of voluntary carve-out plans. The percentage of the Japanese labor force participating in voluntary carve-out plans has declined from a peak of 40 percent in the mid-1990s to 18 percent in 2004 (Takayama 2005). Thus, as in the United Kingdom, there has been a large decline in the percentage of the workforce participating in voluntary carve-outs.

---

the carve-out and will have a long-run effect on social security finances, which could be either positive or negative. Since it is expected that the U.S. Treasury will pay, on average, a real rate of return of 3 percent on its bonds that are issued specially for Social Security and are held in the Social Security Trust Fund (President's Commission 2001), the rates of 2.0 and 2.5 percent for determining the reduction in Social Security benefits imply that the individual accounts would be subsidized by the Social Security system.

The carve-out is like a long-term loan to a worker from the social security system. The worker borrows from future social security benefits, with the loan being the reduction in social security contributions. Workers receive the rate of return actually earned on their individual accounts, which would be an expected 3 percent real (but with some interest risk) if they were to invest in Treasury bonds. Workers repay the loan through reduced receipt of social security benefits at the rate specified by the carve-out. If that rate were 2 percent real, workers would receive a government subsidy of 1 percent per year on the balance in their individual account because they would effectively be borrowing from the government at 2 percent and receiving a rate of return of 3 percent on the investment of this borrowing. If the rate were 3 percent, as proposed by President Bush, there would be no expected subsidy over the long term.

A risk-free interest rate is credited to workers' hypothetical accounts for determining the benefit offset since it is presumably applied to the account with certainty, while the investment earnings they actually receive on their accounts are risky. Whether workers take the voluntary carve-out would depend on three factors: how risk-averse they are, what other investments they have, and what special tax incentives, if any, the government would provide.

The Structure of the Trade-Off between Contributions and Benefits

For a voluntary carve-out account, the trade-off between reduced contributions to social security and reduced benefits from it can be structured in various ways. For example, the cut in benefits can be the same percentage as that in the worker's social security contributions. If social security contributions by the worker are reduced by x percent, the future benefits accrued during that period are also reduced by x percent. The reduction in social security benefits with a carve-out can be set as an equal percentage for all workers choosing to take the carve-out. This way may be the simplest administratively.

Age neutrality

An additional complexity in designing carve-outs involves making the reduction in social security benefits age-neutral. With age neutrality, if a worker finds it optimal to take the voluntary carve-out at one age, the worker will find it optimal to continue opting out at older ages. This desirable, conceptually simple feature is difficult to achieve because of the difference in accrual patterns between traditional defined benefit social security plans and individual accounts.

For defined benefit plans and individual accounts that are equally generous at retirement, generally the individual account accrues benefits more rapidly for workers at young ages while the defined benefit plan accrues benefits more rapidly for workers at older ages. This happens because defined benefit plans tend to be backloaded in their patterns of benefit accruals. These different patterns of accrual create an incentive for workers to take the voluntary carve-out when young but not when ıder. The problem of switching incentives can be addressed by making the choice of a carve-out irrevocable. However, such an arrangement raises issues of equity if the terms of the trade-off are subsequently amended, which they almost certainly would be. The British system gives workers greater freedom of choice, allowing workers to switch in or out once a year.

Rather than having a single rebate rate for all workers, the United Kingdom has an array of age-related rates. The rebate is the amount that is deposited in the individual account for workers taking the voluntary carve-out. Younger workers receive lower rebates on their payroll taxes (known as National Insurance contributions) than do older ones since individual accounts of equal lifetime generosity are more favorable than defined benefit plans for younger workers because of the differing accrual patterns. This difference generally occurs between accrual patterns in individual accounts and those in defined benefit plans. In 2001–2002, a 20-year-old received a 4 percent rebate, while a 50-year-old received the maximum rebate of 9 percent. Age-related rebates designed to keep the contracting-out arrangements age-neutral are complex, expensive to administer, and probably poorly understood by workers.

The rebate's size is generally not fixed in a voluntary carve-out system but can be expected to be revised over time. The rebate structure in the United Kingdom is reevaluated by the Government Actuary every five years to take into account increases in life expectancy and changes in interest rates. The rebates have been calculated based on the expense in the private sector of providing a replacement benefit, with an amount added to the rebate as an incentive to take it.

Gender neutrality

A further problem in designing voluntary carve-out individual accounts is to structure the trade-off so that it is gender-neutral. Because women have a longer life expectancy than men, a gender-blind trade-off will not be gender-neutral in effect. The trade-off in the United Kingdom is not gender-neutral, but it encourages men and women to take the voluntary carve-out at different ages. For example, in the late 1990s, 93 percent of eligible men in Britain aged 45–54 chose the individual account, whereas only 32 percent of eligible women in that age group did so (Whitehouse 1998). For many years, Japan structured its voluntary carve-out with different rebates for men and women, but, now that views of gender equity have changed, that is no longer the case (Turner and Watanabe 1995). An additional issue relates to the way changes in life expectancy affect benefits in a voluntary carve-out account and in social security.

In sum, voluntary carve-out accounts are complex to design and to operate. It is difficult to set, in a cost-neutral and nondistorting way, the relationship between contributions to the carve-out accounts and the reduction in the worker's social security benefits. Further, that drop in social security benefits means that the worker's base benefit is decreased, because social security provides the basic benefits in the retirement income system.

MANDATORY INDIVIDUAL ACCOUNTS AROUND THE WORLD

About 30 countries have made individual accounts part of their social security system. This section discusses the features of mandatory individual accounts in selected countries around the world.

South America and the Caribbean

Twelve countries in South and Central America and the Caribbean have incorporated individual accounts into their social security programs (Gill, Packard, and Yermo 2005). In all except Chile's example, the reforms have resulted in workers paying higher mandatory contributions for retirement income plans. The countries adopting individual accounts copied some features of the landmark Chilean reform but diverged in other respects.

Three approaches have been taken (Mesa-Lago 1997). First, directly following Chile's example, the countries of Bolivia, El Salvador, and Mexico have closed their social security systems to new entrants and substituted a mandatory individual account system (mandatory full carve-out). All other reformed countries in Latin America have retained their traditional social security system in some respect.

Second, Uruguay has introduced a mixed system. All workers participate in both a mandatory social security program, which was reduced during the reform but is still dominant, and a mandatory individual account program (partial replacement or mandatory partial carve-out). Because of considerations about financial risk, low-income workers only participate in the traditional social security program.

Third, Colombia and Peru have two competing programs, in which workers either choose the government-run system or a substitute, privately managed plan.

Chile

Because the Chilean reform has been a model for other countries, it is considered here in more detail. Although the main features of the initial Chilean reform are well known in the pension world, the Chilean system has evolved through frequent legislated changes, so that it continues to be a leader in the area of social security reform. The Chilean reform is based on the Chicago School (derived from the University of Chicago) or neoliberal economic principles of free choice, private ownership rights to social security benefits, and private sector investment and administration of pension accounts through competition in the marketplace.

In 1981, Chile reformed its social security system in a way that revolutionized thinking about social security. It became the first country to replace its publicly managed pay-as-you-go defined benefit system with privately managed individual accounts. In the new system, private corporations, known as Administradoras de Fondos de Pensiones (AFPs) or Pension Fund Administrators, manage the investment of the funds.

Workers are required to contribute 10 percent of their pretax salary, up to a ceiling, to a private pension fund of their choosing. The ceiling is indexed, rising monthly at the rate of inflation. Workers can also make voluntary contributions, though few do. An additional amount—ranging from 2.50 to 3.74 percent of a worker's earnings—is levied to finance disability benefits, preretirement survivor benefits, and for general administrative expenses, including a commission. Contributions are withheld by employers from employee pay and transferred monthly to the AFP of the worker's choosing. These payments are tax deductible. Thus, the government subsidizes pensions through the tax system. Employers do not contribute.

The Chilean mandatory pension system began with 12 AFPs and reached a high of 23, but the number has declined, so that in 1999 there were eight, and in 2005 there were six. Most of the reductions in AFPs have resulted from mergers, allowing workers to maintain their account with the merged AFP.

Initially, each AFP could offer only a single fund, but that limit was raised with the addition of a low-risk fund for older workers in response to criticism that the system placed too much financial market risk on workers nearing retirement. Since August 2002, employees have had a further expanded range of investment funds to choose from. The new law allows employees to select one of five funds offered by the AFP. The five fund types are denoted as A through E, going from highest to lowest risk. Men aged 56 and older and women aged 51 and older are prohibited from investing in Fund A. Retirees are limited to investing in one of the three funds with the lowest level of risk (C, D, and E).

The default for participants not choosing an investment is an important feature of an individual account. In Chile, rather than having a single default, employees who fail to make a selection are assigned to a fund according to their age, with older employees being defaulted to a lower-risk fund:

- Fund B—up to age 35 for both males and females,
- Fund C—ages 36–55 for males and ages 36–50 for females, or
- Fund D—age 56 and over for males; age 51 and over for females.

Fund A (for men up to age 55 and women up to age 50) and Fund E (no age limits) are not used for defaults. The younger age limits for females than males for fund types C and D reflect the fact that females are able to retire at younger ages than males: females may retire at age 60 and males may retire at age 65 with an old-age pension. Workers can take their retirement at younger ages if they have saved enough in their accounts to meet government-set minimum standards.

Even though the Chilean pension system is privatized, meaning that it has private sector management, the government still maintains a large role in the retirement income system. For workers contributing for at least 20 years, the system provides a guaranteed minimum benefit. For workers contributing for fewer years, the government provides an anti-poverty benefit. If an AFP is unable to provide the minimum mandatory rate of return, the government terminates the AFP and guarantees the minimum rate of return.

Proponents of the Chilean model claim that its advantages stem from its adherence to free market principles. It gives workers clearly defined property rights in their pension contributions. These rights are believed to decrease the political risks to social security—that government will legislate changes that will reduce the value of the benefits. It provides individual choice as to pension fund manager. It "acts as an engine of, not an impediment to, economic growth; and enhances personal freedom and dignity" (Rodriguez 1999). However, the "ownership society" has not proven to be universally popular in Chile; many workers do not contribute to the system.

Asia

Few Asian countries have used individual accounts for social security. Under the "two systems, one country" policy, Hong Kong maintains a separate social security system from the rest of China. In 2000, it began a mandatory individual account system under which workers and employers both contribute 5 percent of wages into funded individual accounts. Workers can voluntarily contribute higher amounts.

As in 401(k) plans, pension fund managers are chosen by employers, and employees can select only from among the funds provided by that manager (Fox and Palmer 2001). Fund managers typically offer several different choices, with a guarantee fund commonly being provided. Some guarantee funds ensure return of capital, while others guarantee a minimum rate of return. Hong Kong also maintains a fund to compensate participants for losses that are due to illegal activities by fund managers. The system in Hong Kong is not multipillar (providing income from more than one source) since the individual account system will be the primary source of retirement income for most workers participating in it.

Central and Eastern Europe and Central Asia

In 1998, Hungary established mandatory individual accounts, requiring contributions of 8 percent, while maintaining a defined benefit plan as the primary system, with that plan receiving contributions of 22 percent. A key difference between the reforms in Hungary and those in Poland is that Hungary made little change in its existing plan, while Poland completely restructured social security, instituting a notional account system.

A notional account system is a hybrid having features of both defined benefit and individual accounts. Hungary maintains an individual account for each worker, as a defined contribution plan would. However, these are called notional accounts because they are solely bookkeeping entities. Each worker's account is credited with contributions and with interest earnings on accumulated account balances, but these credits are not tied to actual investments. The plan may be run on a pay-as-you-go basis, or it may have investments managed in the same way as defined benefit plans.

Russia has introduced funded individual accounts (Turner and Guenther 2005). Beginning in 2004, 4 percent of the employer's contributions could be paid to private funds rather than to the State Pension Fund. That percentage increases to 6 percent in 2006 (Sandul 2002).

OECD Countries

Unlike in other OECD countries, the basic social security benefit in Australia is income-tested and asset-tested. About 70 percent of retirees receive it. An income-tested benefit is a benefit that workers must qualify for by proving that their income falls below a set level. Australia has never had an earnings-related social security program.

To supplement the income-tested benefit, Australia has introduced a privatized retirement income system, called the Superannuation Guarantee. That system mandates private sector employer-provided pensions that are primarily individual accounts. The contribution rate is 9 percent of salary. Because the government pension is unfunded, the change represents a move toward a funded system.

Because contributions are enforced by legislation and paid into funds administered and invested by the private sector, the Australian government has introduced extensive safeguards to ensure that employees' pension entitlements are secure. This regulation has resulted in increased complexity, added costs, and a heavy burden on trustee boards responsible for overseeing the funds' management.

Sweden has instituted a mandatory individual account system that incorporates lessons learned from the experiences of Chile and other countries, particularly in ways to reduce administrative costs. This individual account system reflects a desire to increase the amount of prefunding in the Swedish retirement income system and place greater emphasis on the role of the capital market and individualism (Harrysson and O'Brien 2003).

In 1999 and 2000, Sweden replaced its traditional defined benefit social security program with a notional account plan supplemented by a mandatory funded individual account. As described earlier, in a notional account system, each worker has an account that is credited with contributions and interest earnings; however, the system is financed on a pay-as-you-go basis, so the individual accounts are not funded, and the balances are bookkeeping entries. Out of a total contribution rate of 18.5 percent of earned income, 16.0 percent is for the notional account system and 2.5 percent is for individual accounts, called the Premium Pension. Starting in 2000, Swedish workers were allowed to choose from 460 different funds to manage their pension investments, with the default being a government-run fund. By 2005, the number of funds exceeded 600.

The Premium Pension system is administered by a new government agency, the Premium Pension Authority (in Swedish, Premipensions-myndigheten, or PPM, as it is known). The PPM acts as a clearinghouse and record keeper for the funded individual account system. This agency was needed because the individual account system includes a broad range of activities that would have been difficult to undertake within the traditional functions of the Swedish Social Insurance Agency. In addition, a central agency is expected to help keep administrative costs low because of scale economies in administration (Palmer 2001).

The United Kingdom encourages contracting-out to individual account plans. While every developed country has a social security system, the United Kingdom is unusual in giving every employer and employee the option of contracting-out of part of social security. Contracting-out in Japan is available on a more limited basis and only through employer-provided defined benefit plans.

Contracting-out in the United Kingdom has developed into a highly complex system. In 1986, the United Kingdom passed an act designed, by using individual accounts, to encourage contracting-out (voluntary carve-outs) from the State Earnings-Related Pension Scheme (SERPS), which is a defined benefit plan. Previously, contracting-out had only been possible with employer-provided defined benefit plans. That law allowed workers to leave SERPS or their employer-provided, contracted-out defined benefit plan by using a personal pension called an Approved Personal Pension. Workers with personal pensions were permitted to recontract into social security (SERPS) if that later appeared to be favorable.

The United Kingdom replaced SERPS with a pension program called the State Second Pension (S2P), which took effect April 2002. Workers and employers are permitted to contract out of the S2P. The S2P has been earnings-related, but in April 2007 it will become a flat-rate benefit, even though contributions are earnings-related. While the S2P is a flat-rate pension, the rebates paid to workers opting out remain connected to earnings. This arrangement provides greater incentive for lower-income earners to stay in the plan and for middle- and higher-income earners to leave.

Employees who contract out receive a rebate on their social security contributions. The amount is intended to reflect the savings to the government from not having to pay the pension to that participant. The money is paid directly into the employee's contracted-out pension fund. Contracting-out has declined in popularity in the United Kingdom; it reached a peak of 69 percent of the workforce in 1991 and had dropped to 61 percent by 2001.

CONCLUSIONS

This chapter presents a broad overview of pension mandating and social security privatization around the world. It discusses issues in the social security reform debate relating to individual accounts and describes the main features of mandated and privatized systems in several countries. Mandating has been far more common an approach than voluntary carve-outs. Some of the complexities of structuring the rebate for a voluntary carve-out are described. The difficulties in designing voluntary carve-outs that are age- and gender-neutral and neutral in their effect on the financing of traditional social security programs are among the reasons few countries have adopted them.

Note

1. These alternatives reflect the fact that different groups within the commission prepared the various proposals.

4

Agency Risk and the Management of Individual Account Investments by Corporations and Mutual Funds

The three-year decline in world stock markets starting in 2000 and the dramatic plunge of technology stock prices made clear that individual account participants face substantial financial market risk. However, participants are also vulnerable to improper management of their investments, as evidenced by the corporate scandals at Enron and WorldCom.

Participants in individual accounts may face risk at three levels of investment management: 1) financial management of corporations, 2) management of investments by mutual funds and other financial intermediaries, and 3) management of investments by individual participants themselves.

Participants in individual accounts must rely on agents—the officers of corporations and the officers of mutual funds. These agents typically have conflicts of interest in that their primary concern may be their own income rather than that of the shareholders. The problems arising when agents manage investments result in agency risk for participants in individual accounts.

In considering financial management by corporations, this chapter examines whether participants in individual accounts have adequate protection. For financial management by mutual funds, the focus is on conflicts of interest in mutual funds, the level of fees participants pay, and the transparency of those fees. The chapter also considers the possible role of government as an investment manager. The following chapter takes up problems arising from financial management by individual participants.

FINANCIAL MANAGEMENT IN MANDATORY
INDIVIDUAL ACCOUNTS

The Swedish Premium Pension system and the Chilean mandatory individual accounts exemplify issues that arise in the institutional management of investments in individual accounts.

The Swedish Premium Pension System

The Swedish Premium Pension system, with its mandatory 2.5 percent contribution, provides individual accounts designed to reduce the administrative burden on employers and to limit advertising costs and administrative expenses for service providers by using centralized management through a government agency. It provides an example of how individual accounts might be managed in the United States.

As mentioned in Chapter 2, the Premium Pension is administered by a government agency established for this purpose, the Premium Pension Authority (PPM). As a clearinghouse and record keeper for the individual accounts, the PPM collects contributions, disburses them to mutual funds, and makes benefit payments. A central agency should help keep administrative costs low because of scale economies (Palmer 2001b).

When considering the administrative costs of pension systems, generally the focus is on the institutions managing the investments and the pension system, and the important issue of the costs borne by employers is ignored. The administrative burden on employers varies greatly by type of individual account. The Premium Pension places a minimal administrative burden on employers. Employers withhold contributions from employees' pay, aggregate the tax and contribution withholdings for their employees, and make a single monthly tax and contribution payment to the National Tax Authority.

Swedish employers only report information on the individual worker's earnings once a year to the government. Therefore, individual pension rights cannot be established until workers have filed the income data for their income taxes and these statements have been consolidated with employers' reports. Collecting contributions and then posting them to the workers' accounts takes the National Tax Authority and the PPM

18–24 months or longer from January of the year in which the contributions were made. When the tax authorities have determined individual pension rights, they inform the PPM as to how much each worker's account should be credited, and the PPM transfers that amount to the workers' accounts.

In the interim before individual workers' pension rights have been established, pension contributions are placed in a fund at the National Debt Office. The rate of return paid on the fund is close to that paid on government debt. Because government bonds in Sweden are secure, they provide a guaranteed rate of return for the Premium Pension participants.

Workers can challenge the income and contribution statements that the tax authorities provide, and errors in record keeping inevitably occur. In December 2001, the National Tax Authority informed the PPM that it had changed income and contribution figures for 50,000 workers (out of approximately 4.5 million). The tax authority had understated the income and therefore the pension contributions for 11,000 people (Reid 2002). This problem raises the issue of whether workers should be compensated for the shortfall in investment income if the shares that should have been credited have appreciated.

When the National Tax Authority has informed the PPM of the amount credited to each worker, workers select how to invest their annual contributions. At the same time, all new labor market entrants allocate their initial contributions to mutual funds. Workers also can elect to place their contributions in their spouse's account instead of in their own. This feature allows spouses to choose a form of earnings sharing to determine their household pension benefits, which can be used, for example, to supplement the account of a wife who is out of the labor force rearing children.

The PPM places all the workers' contributions for a year, plus the accumulated interest, in the mutual funds over a period of four to five days. For example, in the second week of April 2001, the PPM received 20 billion Swedish crowns (SEK), the contributions from 1999 (Jarvenpaa 2001). In the first week of February 2002, the PPM placed approximately SEK20 billion from the funds into the Swedish Premium Pension system, which was the amount of the contributions plus interest for the year 2000 (PPM 2002). Thus, the system treats all workers equally with regard to the timing of the investment of their contributions in the

mutual funds. Workers can make daily interfund transfers of money already invested except during the blackout period, when the annual contributions are being placed.

The PPM keeps all records of the individual accounts and fund share values. It aggregates individual transactions concerning interfund transfers at the PPM at the end of each day and then transmits a net purchase or redemption to each fund. The PPM matches buy and sell orders internally, limiting its transactions with fund managers to the net amount of the individual transactions. This procedure greatly reduces the mutual funds' transaction costs compared to a system in which mutual funds receive contributions for and make benefit payments to individual participants.

A system design issue is the number of choices an individual account system offers to workers. One view posits that the greater the range and number of options, the better able are workers to make a selection that suits their personal situation. An alternative position is that, beyond a point, more choices raise the likelihood of errors in decision making by individuals lacking a sophisticated understanding of investments.

Swedish workers have far more investment choices than do participants in any other type of mandatory individual account. Initially in 2000, the Premium Pension offered a choice of 455 mutual funds; by 2005, that number had risen to more than 600. More than 80 mutual fund companies participate in the system; nearly half of these companies are managed outside Sweden.

Swedes have shown a strong preference for domestically managed funds, with foreign funds receiving only 4 percent of all contributions (Weaver 2002). This suggests that many participants have chosen mutual fund companies with which they are familiar, rather than trying to evaluate the choices.

One reason for allowing participants to select from among numerous funds, including international ones, is that the Swedish stock market is small; if only a few domestic funds were available, they eventually would dominate the market. Any mutual fund company licensed in Sweden may participate in the Premium Pension system. Generally, licensed funds must meet the European Union's portfolio diversification requirements. Swedish equity funds, however, are exempt because the Swedish equity market is dominated by one company, Ericsson (Weaver 2002).

The PPM provides participants with a booklet that lists all available funds. Further, it provides this listing without charge to the funds, which results in free advertising to those interested in the Swedish market. For this reason, it would appear desirable to charge a flat fee for companies to participate, reducing substantially the number of funds with few investors.

The booklet divides the funds into categories and subcategories, including domestic and international stock funds, mixed stock-bond funds, and bond funds. Derivatives funds are considered to be too risky an investment for social security accounts and thus are not included as an option.

Most of the funds are equity funds; of these, about 10 percent are index funds, investing passively in a broad stock market index rather than actively researching and picking securities. Index funds tend to have the lowest fees of any funds because they are passively managed: there is no fee for paying analysts to study stocks and make subsequent buy and sell decisions since those activities are not undertaken. Passively managed funds also have low portfolio turnover costs because they do relatively little trading.

Participants can invest in bonds through about 70 bond funds in addition to about 80 generation funds. The mix of stocks and bonds in these funds varies with the participants' age; the percentage held in bonds increases with age so that older workers hold less risky portfolios. One-quarter of the funds invest primarily in Sweden.

In addition to a wide range of domestic and foreign funds, Swedish workers also can invest in one of two government-managed funds. A government organization, the Seventh Swedish National Pension Fund, is the default fund for workers who do not make their own choice. It manages the money for those workers who do not choose a fund or funds. This fund has more than three times as many participants as the fund most frequently designated by choice (PPM 2002). As of 2002, the default fund held about 30 percent of the assets invested in the Premium Pension system, and roughly 40 percent of the participants invested in it.[1] The second government fund is an alternative for workers who want the government to manage their individual account. To participate in this fund, workers must specify it.

The Seventh Swedish National Pension Fund (Sjunde AP-fonden, or Seventh AP Fund, or AP7) manages both funds with an independent, appointed board that functions as a fund manager. The default fund is heavily invested in equity. Its equity holdings cannot exceed 90 percent of the total value in this fund or fall below 80 percent. Of the equity holdings, as much as 75 percent can be invested in foreign stocks. In 2001, the default fund invested 90 percent of its assets in Swedish and international equities. In 2002, that figure had declined to 82 percent in equities, of which 17 percent were in Swedish holdings and 65 percent were in foreign ones (Sjunde AP-fonden 2003b, p. 4).

The Swedish default fund has a much riskier portfolio than is typical of default funds in 401(k) plans with automatic enrollment of participants. Those default funds—presumably at least in part because of worries over legal liabilities if losses are incurred—typically consist of fixed-income securities. Part of the Swedish default fund is managed actively, and part is managed passively, invested in broad indexes. Part of the fund's passive portion is invested in an indexed bond fund.

One concern with funded mandatory pensions is the risk of political interference by government in investment decisions and capital markets. The broad range of funds and few limitations on the choices of funds offered in the Swedish system greatly reduce the concern that the government may manipulate the investment process or limit the range of investment choice on political grounds.

An issue that arises with government management of pension investments is whether investment decisions should take social issues into account rather than be based solely on financial considerations of risk, liquidity, and expected return. The two Swedish government funds' investment strategies incorporate environmental and ethical concerns. The funds invest only in companies that adhere to the international conventions Sweden has signed on human rights, child labor, the environment, and corruption. They will not invest in companies that have violated United Nations human rights standards, child labor standards, International Labor Organization standards concerning the treatment of workers, and international conventions against bribery, corruption, and environmental degradation. These restrictions on investments do not apply to nongovernment-managed funds, although some voluntarily follow them.

Because of these restrictions, the Swedish government funds do not invest in some large, well-known companies. The government funds invest in between 2,000 and 2,500 companies worldwide, and during summer 2001, the government funds screened all of these companies for adherence to the standards. The results indicated that approximately 30 companies violated the conventions, so they were excluded from the portfolio.[2] While the funds' policy only excludes companies that have violated international conventions, broken laws, or admitted wrongdoing, companies that have been banned on that basis include the Coca-Cola Company, Exxon Mobil Corporation, Liz Claiborne, and Sears, Roebuck and Company, according to the Seventh Swedish National Pension Fund's (AP7) annual report (Sjunde AP-fonden 2003a, pp. 19–20). Because most new workers entering the system are in the default fund, they are not investing in Coca-Cola and these other prominent companies. This raises a question of whether participants are sacrificing rate of return for social goals.

Marketing costs have added greatly to the expense of mandatory individual accounts in some countries, as discussed later in this chapter. To avoid that problem, in Sweden the mutual fund management companies participating in the system know the total investment from the Premium Pension but not the identities of individual investors. Because fund managers do not know their clients, it is expected that entry costs to the Swedish market would be reduced for non-Swedish funds. Mutual funds only need to offer investment management services; they do not need to spend money acquiring distribution channels, which means they do not need to hire numerous sales agents and open retail offices (Herbertsson, Orszag, and Orszag 2000).

While the investment returns earned by individual accounts may have a large effect on their popularity, it is not reasonable to judge a well-managed system by such returns, because a pension system cannot earn better rates of return than are available in the capital markets. Because of world equity markets' decline during the period 2000–2002, many funds earned negative rates of return over this period. The total return for the AP7 Fund, the default fund, was −7.4 percent in 2000, −10.6 percent in 2001, and −26.7 percent in 2002. This compares to a total return for the PPM index (the capital-weighted average for all PPM system funds open for active choice) of −10.6 percent in 2001 and

−33.1 percent in 2002 (Sjunde AP-fonden 2003b). (The figure for 2000 is not available.)

The Chilean System

Chile's mandatory individual accounts provide further evidence as to issues encountered in investment management. Chile permits firms to freely enter into and exit from the pension fund administration (AFP) market, even of foreign companies, provided that minimum capital requirements are met. The AFPs compete for participants. Workers are free to select the AFP of their choice, and for a number of years they could switch their accounts among pension providers as often as they wished. Since 1997, participants have only been able to change AFPs after meeting a minimum stay requirement of six months, a restriction implemented to decrease administrative costs that resulted from frequent shifts in AFPs by some workers. This policy limits free choice but appears to eliminate excessive changing of AFPs by some participants. This activity was driven by the commissions the AFP sales force received for attracting new members and by incentives, such as small appliances, provided to participants to induce them to switch. The Swedish Premium Pension system, by contrast, has no minimum stay requirement, but it also does not have a sales force marketing to individual participants and trying to entice them to switch funds.

The AFPs have a high proportion of Chilean pension assets in government bonds. This figure generally has been around 40 percent of the assets in the system, but it reached a peak of 47 percent in 1986 (Rodriguez 1999). The large percentage of pension investments in Chilean government bonds appears to be counter to the philosophy of the Chilean free enterprise model of investing in the private sector.

TIERS OF FINANCIAL MANAGEMENT

Several issues have arisen concerning investor protections in the first two of the three tiers of pension investment management: financial management by corporations and by mutual funds.

Tier One: Corporations

Financial market scandals during the early years of the twenty-first century raised questions as to whether pension participants, along with other investors in financial markets, had adequate protections in U.S. capital markets against conflicts that arise from the separation of corporate ownership and control.

Conflicts of interest in corporations

The collapse of Enron Corporation and other corporate scandals exposed weaknesses in the safeguards that protect U.S. investors. Arthur Andersen LLP, the external accounting and auditing firm hired by Enron, did not detect and correct inaccuracies in Enron's financial statements. Enron's board of directors did not prevent the company from distorting its financial statements. Thus, investors relied on false financial statements. Even though the accounting firm and the board of directors are supposed to act independently to protect the interests of investors, including pension participants whose individual accounts are invested in the company, they both are employed by the company. Because of this conflict of interest, they may be reluctant to thwart top management's wishes.

The quality of information contained in financial disclosures

Because of bad accounting, Enron was able to conceal billions of dollars of liabilities so that its financial position appeared to be much more favorable than it actually was. This raises the issue of whether the laws governing financial disclosures by corporations, and their enforcement, are adequate.

Analysts on Wall Street and the credit rating firm that evaluated Enron failed to detect problems and may have failed to adequately investigate Enron's finances before advising investors. They have argued in their defense that they relied on the accounting information that was available. Nonetheless, financial analysts face potential conflicts of interest: gaining investment banking business for their firms, preserving good relations with the companies they cover, and supplying buy rather than sell recommendations to the mutual fund industry (Baer and Gensler 2002). These potential conflicts cast doubt on the usefulness of information provided by some financial analysts and credit rating firms.

Compounding problems concerning the quality of financial information, two large banks were implicated in the fall of Enron Corporation for hiding billions of dollars in loans. The concealment made it appear that Enron had less debt than was actually the case. While not admitting guilt, the banks paid millions of dollars in fines to the Securities and Exchange Commission (SEC).

Even with full, accurate, and transparent disclosure of relevant financial information, corporations may not be good stewards of their shareholders' funds. They may overpay their top executives, paying millions of dollars a year for the management of even poorly run corporations. Or they may disburse funds in ways that are counter to at least some shareholders' interests (such as by donating to the political campaigns of particular candidates or to charities).

Tier Two: Mutual Funds

Because individual account participants generally invest in mutual funds rather than in individual stocks, the second tier of management affecting investment value for individual account participants concerns mutual funds and pension fund management companies. Conflicts of interest arise in the management of mutual funds just as they do in the management of corporations (Mahoney 2004).

Preferential treatment

In 2003, the New York State Attorney General charged that at least one U.S. mutual fund provided preferential treatment to some investors. These individuals were allowed to trade after the market had closed, based on the market closing price. Thus, these investors could benefit from information that became available after market closing that would affect the price of the mutual fund. This illegal practice allowed some investors to benefit at the expense of others.

Does competition reduce costs?

The designers of the Chilean system thought that market competition would ensure the lowest possible administrative costs as pension fund providers competed for participants on the basis of fees. To encourage competition by permitting free movement of workers between funds, the Chilean pension fund management companies, or AFPs, are not permitted to charge exit fees when workers change AFPs.

Commissions charged by the AFPs in Chile are set competitively, meaning that their level is not regulated by the government. However, there is little price competition in commissions, because no AFP advertises that it offers low fees. Instead, advertising focuses on the service provided or on building a brand image, such as for financial stability. In addition, AFPs have offered financial incentives to workers to switch companies. This type of competition has not led to the free market result expected, that of reduced fees. Instead, high expenses relating to advertising and marketing have increased costs. The sales force in the system rose from 3,500 in 1990 to 15,000 in 1995 (OECD 1998).

In the United Kingdom, competitive forces alone were also not sufficient to drive down charges on retail financial products. As a result of this apparent market failure, the government introduced individual account Stakeholder plans in 2001, subject to a statutory maximum annual charge of 1 percent of asset values, with no entry or exit charges. Because of this regulatory limit, providers of Stakeholder pensions have greatly reduced the amount of "free" advice they provide to workers trying to decide whether to choose these accounts (Bolger 2001). Some insurance companies have argued that a cap on fees of 1 percent for an individually marketed financial product is too low and have decided not to offer it. The fee cap has since been raised to 1.5 percent for the first 10 years of an account, after which it can be no more than 1.0 percent. One of the reasons for the high level of fees is that providers of these pensions must determine whether they are an appropriate investment for the individuals who participate.

The costs of maintaining a financial account are largely fixed, not varying by the size of the balance. Consequently, financial institutions often charge flat fees for maintaining accounts, which fall especially heavily on low-income workers because of their relatively small account balances. In part because of the fixed charges, Australia has exempted low-income workers from mandatory individual accounts. This exemption is similar to the practice in Denmark, which excludes those who work less than 10 hours a week from the mandatory individual accounts.

Comparative administrative costs

The operation of the Swedish Premium Pension system differs from that of most other mandatory individual accounts. Sweden has tried to reduce costs by implementing a central agency to manage the accounts. This approach raises the question of whether the Swedish system has lower administrative costs than the system in Chile or the one in the United Kingdom.

The administrative costs in the Chilean system in 1998 averaged 1.36 percent of account balances. Chile currently has the lowest administrative costs, as a percentage of assets, of any Latin American mandatory pension system, according to one study, because of its large base of assets and longer experience (James, Smalhout, and Vittas 2002). Administration costs tend to fall as assets grow; this is due to economies of scale and learning by doing.

In Sweden, even when the 0.30 percent fee paid to the PPM (the government management agency) is included, a substantial portion of the money contributed to this new system has been invested in funds where the administrative expenses are about half that in Chile.

Participants in Sweden generally have picked low-fee funds: in 2000, 48 percent of the money invested in the system was put in funds with fees ranging from 0.25 to 0.49 percent (Palmer 2001b). Thus, with the addition of the 0.30 percent fee paid to the PPM, nearly half of the money in the system was invested in funds with total fees ranging from 0.55 percent to 0.79 percent, compared to average fees in Chile of 1.36 percent. The total fee in Sweden averaged 0.95 percent of assets in 2000 (Palmer 2001b) and was 0.85 percent in 2001 for nongovernment funds (Engström and Westerberg 2003). The fee paid by participants in the default fund, which was the option in which the most money was invested, was only 0.17 percent in 2002, resulting in a total fee of 0.47 percent (Engström and Westerberg 2003).

The total fees (including the PPM fee) in Sweden are similar to those for large, actively managed mutual funds in the United States but higher than those for passively managed U.S. funds. For example, the Vanguard Group offers passively managed equity funds with annual fees about half those paid in Sweden—less than 0.20 percent of account balances. Fees may tend to be lower in large countries than in small ones, however, because of economies of scale in administrative costs.

The PPM employs a little more than 200 people to run the system. That number does not include the employees of the mutual funds. Because the United States is roughly 30 times larger than Sweden in population, the experience of the PPM implies that a government bureaucracy of more than 6,000 people would be needed to run a similar system in the United States.

The 0.30 percent fee participants pay to the PPM in Sweden is intended to permit the organization to become self-financed over the long run. However, the PPM had to borrow from the government because of high start-up costs, so the reported PPM fee understated the actual initial expenses. Two offsetting effects are expected on future fees. Authorities anticipate that the end of the start-up period, coupled with growth in the accounts, will reduce expenses relative to the asset base. Conversely, the increase in expenses for annuitizing benefits and providing benefit payments will cause fees to rise. On net, the PPM expects its fee to fall.

The fees for the Chilean system do not include the cost of annuitizing benefits or making other forms of benefit payments. The fees in Sweden also basically do not cover this cost because the system is new and few people are claiming benefits. A potentially major difference in administrative expenses between Sweden and Chile is the cost of annuitization. In Sweden, there is no separate fee for annuitizing an account, which is mandatory and is done through the PPM. The average fee for annuitizing in Chile as of 1999, for those workers choosing that option, was 5.25 percent of the account balance (SAFP 2001). An earlier study calculated the fee based on the difference between the rate of return from buying a Chilean 20-year Consumer Price Index–linked bond and the average internal rate of return paid to annuitants; it found that benefits were reduced by 10.20 percent (Valdés-Prieto 1994). The percentage taken by the fee may decrease over time as the size of the account balance being annuitized increases.

The United Kingdom's decentralized individual accounts are particularly expensive; the high cost led the British government to develop Stakeholder pensions. A U.K. study found that the costs of switching funds decreased account balances by about 15 percent on average. The costs of annuitizing benefits trimmed the value of benefits received by about 10 percent. Taking into consideration all costs borne by workers, the value of benefits was cut by 40 to 45 percent (Murthi, Orszag, and

Orszag 2001). These figures do not include the costs of the government agency supervising the system, which are not charged to workers but are borne out of general government revenue.

Thus, the British approach is more costly than that of Chile. The Swedish system is the least expensive in terms of administration, while the costs of large, passively managed U.S. equity funds are even less. A Swedish-type model operated in the United States could result in lower fees than in Sweden because the large size of the U.S. labor market would allow for greater economies of scale in mutual fund management. Including the cost of providing annuitized benefits, fees of about 0.5–0.6 percent of assets might be feasible.

TRANSPARENCY IN INDIVIDUAL ACCOUNTS AND THE DISCLOSURE OF FEES

"Transparency" refers to participants receiving clear information that is adequate to allow them to make informed choices. Transparency is desired in financial transactions, including those in retirement income systems. The transparency of competing methods of providing social security benefits is an issue in the reform debate. Proponents of individual accounts have argued that those accounts are transparent while defined benefit plans are not (World Bank 1994). They view individual accounts as being transparent because the cost to workers, measured as the amount that participants contribute, is clearly identified, as is the amount accumulated in their individual accounts. Furthermore, benefits received are based on the returns on the individual accounts, and those accounts do not involve the transfer of resources across persons. With defined benefit social security systems, workers may have difficulty understanding who is helped from the resource transfers across different groups of participants.

Individual account participants need transparency so that they can compare the fees of different mutual funds or pension funds. Competition concerning fees will not occur if participants do not know how much they are being charged. Transparency may lead to competitive pressures on service providers to reduce fees, and individual participants would be better able to judge the performance of their pension service provider and to understand the effect of fees on their accumulation of assets. Inadequate disclosure may be a factor in the large variance in charges and expenses of 401(k) plans (Economic Systems Inc. 1998). What appears to be a small difference in fees can mean thousands of dollars to a worker over the life of an individual account.

Ensuring that greater information is provided to consumers, when balanced against the costs of providing that data, generally is considered to be a legitimate activity of government, rather than an intrusive extension of regulatory powers. The issues concerning social security's transparency have three components: expenditures, benefits, and the relationship between expenditures and benefits (Table 4.1). Expenditures have two components: mandatory contributions and fees. This section, based on the research of Korczyk and Turner (2003), examines the transparency of the fees charged participants in individual accounts. It addresses the question: Do participants know how much they are paying in fees and expenses on their individual accounts? The focus is on fees incurred during the accumulation phase before retirement.

Types of Individual Account Fees

Individual account fees include those charged by plan administrators and fund managers and transaction costs for security purchases and sales. Fees reflect administration costs: collecting contributions, keeping records, communicating with participants, educating participants about financial matters, preparing reports for the government, complying with ongoing government requirements, updating plans to maintain

Table 4.1 Issues in Pension Transparency for Social Security Systems

Components	Defined contribution	Defined benefit
Costs	Disclosure of fees	Uncertain future costs
Benefits	Depends on financial markets	May be affected by politics
Relationship between costs and benefits	Unclear effect of fees on level of future benefits	Benefit formulas may make relationship complex

SOURCE: Author's compilation.

Table 4.2 The Structure of Fees in a Mixed (Equity Bond) Mutual Fund

Fees and expenses[a]	Amount ($ 000s)
Investment advisory services	20,725
Distribution services	20,028
Transfer agent services	5,676
Administrative services	999
Custodian	708
Registration statement and prospectus	675
Postage, stationery, and supplies	643
Reports to shareholders	235
State and local taxes	116
Directors' compensation	106
Auditing and legal	69
Other	97
Total	50,104
Total assets	15,914,561

NOTE: Figures in the source are unaudited.
[a] For the six months ending April 30, 2003.
SOURCE: American Funds Capital Income Builder (2003).

compliance with changing legal requirements, and disbursing benefits (Table 4.2). Charges also arise from the cost of managing investments: the bid-ask spread in the buying and selling of financial assets, as well as transaction costs and fees for researching alternative investments.

Some fees can be allocated to different participants based on their cost-generating activities, or the fees can be spread over all participants. Charges can be front-loaded, meaning that they are paid at the same time as contributions, or they can be back-loaded and charged on exit. They can be imposed as a flat annual rate, annually as a percentage of assets or contributions, or itemized based on fee-generating activities. Some of the largest fees are completely hidden. Brokerage commissions are included in the cost of shares (raising their cost) and are not broken out as separate fees in shareholder reports (Norris 2003). The essential issue, however, is the need for funds to disclose in a readily understandable manner the aggregate amount of fees charged against the assets or contributions to an individual's account. In that way, the participant can make an informed decision when choosing among funds.

Survey of Transparency in Individual Account Fees

Transparency in individual accounts depends on how and to what extent participants receive information about the fees they pay. The following discussion explains how this issue is addressed in the United States, Australia, Chile, Sweden, and the United Kingdom.

The United States' Thrift Savings Plan

The Thrift Savings Plan provides individual accounts for U.S. federal government workers that are similar to 401(k) plans for private sector workers. It is one of the largest pension plans in the world. Participants receive statements, which provide information as to beginning assets, contributions, withdrawals, investment earnings, change in market value, and ending assets. While the statements appear to give a complete accounting of inflows and outflows determining the difference between beginning and ending assets, they provide no information about the amount by which participants' accounts have been reduced by fees. Information about the calculation of fees is contained in descriptions of the plan, but nowhere can the participant find the total amount that he or she paid. In addition, fees arising from transactions costs in the purchase and sale of securities are not disclosed. These fees are hidden in the net investment returns. It would be more transparent to separate gross investment returns from fees (Box 4.1).

401(k) plans

Like the Thrift Savings Plan, 401(k) plans do not disclose to participants the total amount in fees charged to them. Under Department of Labor (USDOL) regulations, a Summary Plan Description must include any provision that may result in the imposition of a fee on a participant (Huss 2003). However, information on the schedule determining the actual amount of fees charged generally is not contained in such documents because the information may differ if service providers are changed. The data may be in the documents of the service providers to the plans. For investments involving mutual funds, the fees on a percentage basis relative to assets are available in the mutual fund prospectuses.

**Box 4.1 Is the Thrift Savings Plan a
Model for Social Security Reform?**

The Thrift Savings Plan is an individual account plan that the federal government provides for its employees. It is a possible model for individual accounts as part of Social Security.

How the Thrift Savings Plan Works

The Thrift Savings Plan is similar to 401(k) plans in the private sector. Federal government employees are not required to contribute, but can contribute up to 14 percent of their pay. The federal government automatically contributes 1 percent of pay for all eligible employees hired since 1983, whether or not they contribute. If workers choose to contribute, it also makes matching contributions. Workers have a choice of five broad-based investment funds, plus a lifecycle fund that automatically shifts its portfolio more into bonds as workers approach their expected retirement date. Workers can withdraw benefits at age 59½ and continue working for the federal government. They can receive loans from their accounts while working. Workers are not required to annuitize their account balances or to provide survivor's benefits. Workers participating in the Thrift Savings Plan also contribute fully to Social Security and in addition have an employer-provided defined benefit plan. Thus, their investments in the Thrift Savings Plan are on top of a solid base of Social Security and a defined benefit pension plan.

**The Thrift Savings Plan as a Model
for Social Security Reform**

Add-on accounts, such as the Thrift Savings Plan, do not reduce traditional Social Security benefits, and they do not worsen the financing of Social Security because they do not affect the contributions paid into it. In these respects, the Thrift Savings Plan may be a good model for Social Security reform.

Box 4.1 (continued)

In some other respects, however, the Thrift Savings Plan has features that may not be a good model for Social Security reform. Workers are allowed to take loans from their accounts while working. They can begin withdrawing from their accounts at age 59½ while working. They can retire at age 57 and begin collecting benefits. These features may reduce the amount that would be available in the accounts for retirement needs at older ages. Also, workers can make interfund transfers daily. That allows some workers to try to time the market, which generally is inappropriate for long-term investing. Workers are not required to annuitize their account balances. Though that feature may be satisfactory for an add-on account because adequate annuitization for federal workers is provided through Social Security and the defined benefit plan, the feature would not be desirable for a carve-out account that reduced Social Security benefits. The benefits provided by the Thrift Savings Plan are not price-indexed, and there is no requirement that survivor's benefits or disability benefits be provided through the plan.

A Department of Labor ruling permits certain fees to be charged to individual accounts based on participants' activities that generate costs, such as requesting a benefit payment (Huss 2003). Thus, fees for some services may be clearly disclosed to participants. However, even plan sponsors may not know how much in fees their participants are being charged for other services, such as those supplied by record keepers, investment managers, and other service providers. This situation arises because plan sponsors have consistently favored the imbedded and invisible mutual fund pricing model, rather than explicitly accounting for and paying for custodial, record keeping, and other services (Rosenblatt 2001).

About one-third of 401(k) assets are invested in mutual funds (Jossi 2003). The SEC regulates mutual funds and prescribes what fees and expenses borne by investors must be disclosed and in what format. By law, mutual funds disclose some fees and expenses in a standardized table near the front of the prospectus. They disclose them as an expense ratio, which is the annual ratio of expenses divided by assets. An individual participant's fee as determined by the expense ratio is debited from the shareholder's assets every month. Pension participants may be charged the expense ratio for retail clients or a lower institutional rate.

Mutual funds are not required to disclose, however, and consequently do not disclose all of the fees and expenses charged to participants' individual accounts. For example, they do not disclose expenses incurred in buying and selling securities. These costs appear to be about 0.5 to 1.0 percent of assets annually for actively managed mutual funds (Baer and Gensler 2002). Under what are called soft dollar arrangements, mutual fund investment advisers use part of the brokerage commissions they pay to broker-dealers for executing trades to obtain research and other services. Because these expenses are not disclosed and the soft dollar costs are combined with transaction charges, this arrangement adds further to the lack of transparency in fees that 401(k) participants bear (USGAO 2003).

The remaining two-thirds of 401(k) funds in the United States not invested in mutual funds are invested in guaranteed investment contracts (GICs), separate insurance company accounts, bank collective funds, and employer stock. Many of these vehicles disclose even less information about fees than do mutual funds. The problem is especially acute in plans operated by insurance companies (Jossi 2003). Typically, fees and expenses on GICs, offered by insurance companies, and on bank deposit accounts are not disclosed to the purchaser; only the net rate of return is provided.

In sum, 401(k) plan participants rarely, if ever, know how much they have paid in fees. Even if they were to try to obtain that information, under current business practices in the financial services sector it would generally not be possible for them to receive a complete accounting of the fees they had been charged (Box 4.2).

Australia

International experience offers useful models for providing transparency in the fees charged to individual account participants. Australia requires mutual funds and pension plans to disclose fees that workers pay. The rule applies both to establishing an account and to providing the periodic statements. Thus, when a pension plan or mutual fund provides a

---

Box 4.2 The Effect of Fees

Given the large variation in the level of fees charged on individual accounts, the effect of fees on benefits at retirement can be substantial. Consider two different situations, both of which involve a worker contributing $1,000 a year to an individual account over a career of 30 years. In the low-fee situation, where fees are 0.2 percent a year, the worker receives a real rate of return of 3 percent. In the high-fee situation, where fees are 1.2 percent a year, the worker receives a real rate of return of 2 percent. After 30 years, the low-fee worker has an account balance of $47,575, while the high-fee worker has an account balance of $40,568. The difference between the account balance of the high-fee worker and that of the low-fee worker is roughly equal to seven years of contributions.

---

report of account activity, which typically includes the opening balance, contributions, withdrawals, investment earnings, gains or losses, and end-of-period balance, it also shows in Australian dollars the amount in fees charged the account holder. Consequently, the system in Australia provides a possible model for the transparent disclosure of fees.

Chile

Pension funds in Chile levy a fixed administrative fee and a charge on contributions (Whitehouse 2001). Because the charge on contributions is in addition to the mandatory payment of 10 percent of earnings, participants are presumably well aware of the fees they are assessed, although they may have little understanding of the impact on their retirement income. This approach is also used by Colombia, El Salvador, and Peru (Bateman 2001). Participants, however, do not know how much they pay in fees arising from the buying and selling of assets by the pension fund providers.

Sweden

The mandatory Premium Pension system in Sweden has a complex fee structure. It charges a fixed annual fee of 0.3 percent of the account balance and a money management fee. The 0.3 percent fee is collected by each mutual fund from the assets that it manages and is transmitted to the PPM, which administers the system, for its expenses.

The money management fee is complex. Each mutual fund charges a management fee. Funds must charge the same money management fees in the Premium Pension system as they charge in retail markets. The fund companies' contracts with the PPM stipulate, however, that some of the fee must be returned to the PPM. The rebate is possible because the PPM performs most of the administrative functions for the accounts, so the fund managers' administrative costs are lower in the Premium Pension system than in retail financial markets.

The PPM passes on to the participants all of the savings from the rebate. An individual participant's rebate consists of two parts: an individual share and a general share. The individual share depends on the fees charged by the funds in which the person has invested and is given for funds whose usual fee exceeds 0.4 percent.[3] Once the individual rebates have been distributed, the remaining rebate is apportioned among all participants based on account size. Because the remaining rebate is tied to the participants' account balances and not to fees paid, it returns a higher percentage of fees to workers choosing low-fee funds.

The mutual fund fee covers all of the fund's expenses except transaction costs arising from its purchase and sale of securities. Those fees are incorporated in the net rate of return the workers receive on their account balances.

Individuals participating in the system receive an annual statement indicating the amount in their accounts in the Premium Pension, and that provides no information on fees paid. Also, individual fund charges are not listed on the annual statements and are only available in percentage terms in the annual catalog of funds provided to participants.

United Kingdom

The United Kingdom requires individual account providers to publish figures showing the impact of their administrative costs on plan account balances. Providers apply a mandated set of assumptions on rates of return and publish what the projected payouts would be after all charges have been imposed. Consequently, this system not only provides information on fees but also indicates the expected effect of these costs on account balances.

GOVERNMENT AS FUND MANAGER

In mandatory individual accounts in some countries, the government acts as a financial manager. For example, the governments in Argentina and Uruguay manage one of the mutual funds. In Sweden, the government manages the default fund and another mutual fund.

The main issue of agency risk that arises is whether the government can be trusted to manage financial assets without basing investment decisions on political criteria. Another issue is that the government may be a high-cost investment manager. The evidence on these issues is mixed. While many of the provident funds in Africa appear to have been poorly managed (World Bank 1994), that finding does not necessarily indicate that government would perform inadequately in other countries.

The Petroleum Fund in Norway, the Quebec Pension Fund in Canada, funds for the Canada Pension Plan, and funds for the social security system in New Zealand appear to be successful examples of government management (Gillion et al. 2000). The two funds managed by government agencies in Sweden have not been criticized for making investment decisions based on political considerations (Turner 2004). Those funds are actively managed by a government board that operates independently.

Examples of good pension fund management by the federal government in the United States include the Pension Benefit Guaranty Corporation (PBGC) and the Thrift Savings Plan. The PBGC is the government corporation that guarantees benefits for U.S. defined benefit plans and actively manages investments. The Thrift Savings Plan, which is like a 401(k) plan for federal government workers, passively manages investments (Gillion et al. 2000).

State government pension plans in the United States are other examples of government management of funds. A survey of investment practices of state government pension funds has noted four possible ways that these funds could try to exert political influence (Munnell, Sundén, and Taylor 2000). First, pension funds could engage in economically targeted investments (ETIs), which are designed to meet some special need within the state. Second, the funds could try to influence the behavior of corporations through shareholder activism. Third, the funds could avoid investments in certain stocks for political reasons.

Fourth, the funds could be used by the state governments as a source of financing, from which they could borrow. This survey concludes that, while in the 1980s some state government pension funds sacrificed returns by making politically motivated investments, in recent years these funds have performed as well as those in the private sector.

CONCLUSIONS

Scandals at Enron and WorldCom have highlighted the risks that U.S. pension participants bear from corporate mismanagement. These scandals exposed major weaknesses in the elaborate system of protection for U.S. investors. Other issues concern compensation of the leadership of U.S. corporations and the use of corporate funds for political purposes.

The Swedish system offers a broad range of investment choices, a feature that increases costs. It has been able to keep expenses relatively low by using centralized administration. It has also attempted to reduce the scope for advertising and has regulated fees. The fee structure is complex but creates incentives for workers to participate in lower-cost funds. The net result of various design elements is that individual accounts in Sweden provide considerably more choice of investment options than those in Chile, while being managed at lower cost.

Individual accounts are generally not transparent in their disclosure of fees, and it would be difficult for participants to obtain that information if they attempted to do so. For example, in the Premium Pension system in Sweden, there is no statement of the total costs paid by individuals. In the Thrift Savings and 401(k) plans in the United States, total fees paid by individual participants are not indicated. In all these cases, participants are charged fees, but they do not know how much they are paying. The Chilean and Australian pension systems, however, have a clear identification and disclosure of fees, although even those systems do not list expenses that arise from the purchase and sale of securities. The United Kingdom has also taken steps to improve the disclosure of fees.

Fee information is usually provided in plan documents or in the prospectus for a financial market instrument. That, however, is not in the most accessible or useful format; it does not disclose transaction expenses and soft dollar costs, and it does not disclose the total dollar amount in fees paid by an individual. Greater transparency in individual accounts would allow participants and plan sponsors to make better-informed decisions. It would facilitate participants' choosing among mutual funds based on the level of fees and would thus result in pressure to lower such charges.

Notes

1. These figures are based on the author's calculations from the Premium Pension Authority (2002).
2. The effect on returns was very small. Simulations done by the fund indicate that the portfolio excluding the 30 companies had a rate of return that was 15 basis points (0.15 percent) lower than the full portfolio.
3. The rebate is 25 percent of the difference between the gross fee and 0.4 percent of assets.

5
Individual Management Risk

In individual accounts, workers are usually responsible for investment decisions. Since they bear the risk associated with their accounts, there is logic to the responsibility being assigned to them. Many workers, however, are uninformed about capital markets and investment theory and lack the interest to learn about these topics. Given the fluctuations in financial markets, learning by doing is more difficult than in many other areas because there is not always a direct relationship between poor planning and an adverse outcome. The considerations involved in investing in such markets can be complex, and some basic issues in individual financial management remain unresolved by financial experts.

While the assumption of economic rationality is generally useful for economic theory, it is not necessarily the best basis for economic policy. Behavioral economists have identified circumstances related to pension investment decisions that cause participants to make poor decisions (Thaler 2005). These circumstances include situations involving a complex problem when the outcome is a long way off and thus feedback is delayed, and when the choice is made infrequently.

Investment mistakes made by unsophisticated (and sophisticated) pension participants include insufficient diversification, excessive trading, market timing, trading after market changes, and holding what would appear to be too much or too little risk when compared to the investment portfolios of professional investors. To provide examples of some of these issues, this chapter examines individual financial management in both the mandatory Premium Pension system in Sweden, which gives workers a wide range of investment choices, and in the voluntary carve-out system in the United Kingdom. The discussion will then turn to why individuals make errors in managing their pension investments.

INDIVIDUAL FINANCIAL MANAGEMENT IN THE SWEDISH PREMIUM PENSION SYSTEM

Participant Investment Choice

Although the PPM, the government agency that is responsible for the Swedish Premium Pension system, has the goal that as many participants as possible actively choose their account investments, a substantial percentage of workers do not pick a mutual fund for the investment of their account, and the PPM puts their contributions in the default fund.

The initial investment choices in the Premium Pension system were made by participants in 2000. Everyone who wanted to make an active decision was required to submit a form to the PPM, and people who did not choose or who wanted their funds to be invested in the government default fund did not have to take any action. About two-thirds of participants submitted the form. Women were somewhat more likely than men to make a selection, as were high-income individuals and participants aged 25–55 (PPM 2001). Investment behavior also varied with the level of contributions. Workers with large contributions were more likely to make an active choice, while about half of participants with low contributions invested in the default fund. Since no action was necessary to invest in the default fund, it is impossible to separate that fund's investors into those who wanted to invest in that option and those who ignored the selection process.

Most new PPM participants, who are all recent entrants into the labor force, do not make investment fund choices. Of the 500,000 new contributors to the system in spring 2001, 325,000 were aged 18 to 27. Only 18 percent of the total chose their funds; the remainder had their contributions invested in the default fund (Betson 2001). The large percentage of new participants who took the default option may be a result of the number of investment choices they were offered: being overwhelmed by the options, they decided to not make a selection, which resulted in their being placed in the default fund. This pattern of large numbers of participants failing to make a choice has been seen, however, in other mandatory individual accounts with far fewer possibilities for investment. In Argentina, for example, 75 percent of the 800,000 new participants in 1999 did not choose a fund and were randomly assigned to one (Grushka 2001). Thus, it appears that many workers do not put a high value on having a choice for their investments.

Traditional economics holds that more choices are always better than fewer because greater choice increases the likelihood that individuals with diverse preferences will find something suitable. Behavioral finance, however, suggests that there can be too many choices, and that when there are, individuals tend to make no selection (Iyengar, Jiang, and Huberman 2004).

Behavioral finance also indicates that, because of worker inertia, the design of default options is important (Madrian and Shea 2001). Workers tend to stay in the default option even though it might not be the best one for them. Rather than the lack of change being purely a result of inertia, however, the default option can be considered as an issue of framing, with some workers viewing this fund as a recommendation by the government as to a reasonable investment. Presumably, workers are more likely to switch out of the default option the more it differs from their optimal choice, though some workers may take a passive approach.

Survey results indicate that many Swedish participants have been confused about the investment process—while 18 percent of new participants in 2001 actually made a choice, 34 percent thought they had. Also, a number of workers indicated that they opted for the default fund because they felt it was safer than other options. That, however, is an inaccurate assessment of its risk (Betson 2001). Another study indicated that the majority of people who made an active choice could not remember which funds they had picked. Of those who made a choice, 73 percent could not name all of the funds they had invested in, and 41 percent could not name any of them (Jarvenpaa 2001).

Of Swedish participants who made a choice, about two-thirds selected equity funds, and half of the money invested was put in equity funds. Because balanced funds, generation funds (in which the portfolio mix changes with a participant's age), and the default fund also invest in equities, taken together more than 80 percent of contributions were put in equities, which is far higher than the traditional advice of 60 percent in equities and 40 percent in bonds. One resulting risk is that workers will be inadequately diversified if they invest solely in the Swedish economy, because of its relatively small size and narrow range of activity, and with its stock market dominated by a few large corporations. The statistics on participants' investments indicate, however, that a majority of workers have some international investments (Weaver 2002).

Workers can invest in a maximum of five funds. On average, they have selected three, but the most common choice was to pick five funds, and only 15 percent of participants who chose a fund chose only one. Because some funds invest in a fairly narrow segment of the stock market, such as high tech, it is possible for participants to invest their entire Premium Pension account so that it has high risk and is poorly diversified.

Plan and Investment Information for Participants

Ensuring that workers receive adequate information is an important aspect of the Swedish government's efforts to help participants make well-informed decisions. Providing sufficient information is especially important because of the large number of investment options employees face. As part of the implementation of the reform, the Swedish Social Insurance Agency undertook a major campaign to educate people. Information about the Premium Pension was part of this effort. The PPM provided additional materials to participants in connection with the investment elections.

The PPM recognizes that people differ in their financial knowledge and their interest in investing. It identifies three groups: 1) motivated participants, mainly high-income males with a college degree and previous investment experience; 2) passive investors, who reported no interest in choosing mutual funds; and 3) those who were interested in choosing mutual funds but reported a lack of knowledge to make investment choices. The PPM estimated that about half of participants were in the third group.

The PPM provides information that targets all three groups. For motivated investors, it is important to provide detailed information on the various funds, whereas for the second and third groups the PPM concentrates on increasing participants' knowledge and motivation. To this end, the PPM provides basic financial information, such as explaining the different types of funds and the value of diversification, as well as more in-depth material on the various choices.

The PPM provides the following basic information about financial markets: over the long term, stocks have had a higher rate of return than bonds, although there is no guarantee that this will continue to be the case. The value of stock funds varies more over time than does the value of bond funds. Although movements in exchange rates affect the value of funds invested abroad and are a source of uncertainty in international investments, foreign investments provide greater risk diversification.

At the start of the system in 2000, the PPM mailed information to workers. It launched a major advertising campaign, which included newspaper advertisements, brochures, and public-service announcements on television and radio. The PPM estimates that the television ads reached 86 percent of participants and that participants saw the ads an average of 12 times. The PPM also organized a series of outreach activities for groups with special needs—for example, immigrants with limited knowledge of the Swedish language and individuals with disabilities.

The Swedish system was designed to reduce marketing costs, which have been high in some countries such as Chile. Because the fund managers do not know the identity of their clients, they are unable to target workers who do not participate in their fund, or to offer incentives to specific people to switch funds. The funds, however, have attempted to target their advertising to particular groups by direct mail or by advertising in certain publications appealing to high-income workers or in specific areas where high-income individuals live.

Before making a choice, every participant receives a catalog, which contains information about each fund's investments, risk level, past returns (for preexisting funds), and fees. The same material is also available on the PPM Web site. All of the background is provided in Swedish as well as in the most common languages of immigrants, including English.

Funds that participate in the system must provide daily information on fund asset values. These statistics are available to participants through the major daily Swedish newspapers, over the Internet, and at social security offices. Individual participants receive a single year-end statement concerning their investments in the Premium Pension, but it does not provide information on the fees they have paid.

INDIVIDUAL INVESTMENT ISSUES IN A VOLUNTARY CARVE-OUT SYSTEM

Although the financial issues in individual accounts such as Sweden's are complicated enough to overwhelm many participants, as evidenced by the large numbers who take the default option, a voluntary carve-out system presents more complexities.

Because of their lack of knowledge and information, participants in individual accounts may seek advice on whether to remain fully in the social security system or to take the voluntary carve-out. Pension service providers with an interest in workers' choosing those accounts may take advantage of this lack of financial sophistication. That problem occurred in the United Kingdom with the pensions "mis-selling" scandal (Gillion et al. 2000). Because many workers possess insufficient knowledge of the markets, regulation should control financial advice that is given in situations where the service providers have a conflict of interest. A conflict of interest may also arise concerning advertising and information given by the financial services industry. Lawsuits may arise over the quality of financial advice, especially when the stock market performs poorly.

With a voluntary carve-out, not only do workers need to understand the fundamentals of investing, as is necessary for other types of individual accounts, but they must also be able to compare the risks and returns of individual accounts with those of traditional social security programs (Box 5.1).

Because a voluntary carve-out reduces a person's retirement income base of social security benefits, workers may invest their individual accounts more conservatively than if the individual account were an add-on to social security. Their choices thus may be more conservative than those of U.S. workers who invest their 401(k) balances. If workers invest more conservatively, the expected returns on their individual accounts will be reduced.

A survey of federal government workers who chose not to participate in the Thrift Savings Plan provides insights as to why workers may not choose a voluntary carve-out from social security. One in six men and women (16 percent) indicated that they did not participate in the Thrift Savings Plan because they did not understand the program,

---

Box 5.1 The Mis-Selling of Individual Accounts

The United Kingdom has established the principle that a worker should only be encouraged to take a voluntary carve-out individual account plan when it is in the best interest of the worker to do so. In violation of that principle, the insurance industry in the United Kingdom has marketed these plans directly to workers, encouraging many workers during the 1990s to take voluntary carve-out plans when it was not in those workers' best interest. This aggressive marketing has led to the mis-selling scandal in the United Kingdom. Because, under the leading proposals in the United States, individual account plans that replaced Social Security would not be marketed directly to individuals by financial service providers receiving commissions for individual sales, the exact form of this scandal would not occur in the United States. Nonetheless, the general problem could occur in that the financial services industry may use advertising to encourage workers to take voluntary carve-outs, even though it would not be in the interest of some of those workers to do so. Similarly, workers may be encouraged to take voluntary carve-outs by some people who have an ideological stake in the choice. Just as many workers in the United Kingdom made bad decisions based on bad advice, many workers in the United States, because of lack of financial sophistication, could end up making bad financial decisions.

---

while 12 percent of men and 15 percent of women reported that they did not participate because they did not have enough information. Ten percent of both men and women indicated that they did not contribute to the plan because they had not gotten around to considering whether to do so, while 14 percent of women and 7 percent of men said that they simply had not bothered to consider whether to participate (Hinz and Turner 1998). Thus, lack of knowledge and inertia may be important reasons for the behavior of people in a voluntary carve-out system.

WHY INDIVIDUALS MAKE ERRORS IN MANAGING
PENSION INVESTMENTS

The discussion now turns to the errors individuals make in managing pension investments. This section draws primarily from U.S. experience and research, surveyed in Turner (2003). Understanding why people make mistakes and the types of errors they make may facilitate the development of policies to protect pension investors from themselves. Regulations may be particularly important if individual accounts are mandated with social security because those accounts then become part of the worker's basic benefits. Some workers have little experience with financial institutions, not even having bank accounts.

A Canadian survey found that workers on average rated choosing the right individual account investment (in Canada the account is known as the Registered Retirement Savings Plan [RRSP] pension) more stressful than going to the dentist (Canadian Press 2005). Nonetheless, not all workers are equally likely to make investment mistakes. Presumably, those who are less sophisticated, educated, and experienced are more likely to make mistakes. Low-income workers with small amounts of money invested in individual accounts may not see a reason to exert effort to gather complex financial information about managing their accounts. These errors can have an important effect on retirement income and thus may affect a retiree's well-being for decades.

An investor error can be defined as a decision made counter to what economic and finance theory indicates is the appropriate choice for a rational person who wants to maximize wealth, given the individual's degree of risk aversion. It is important to distinguish between investor errors and bad luck. Also, while investor errors over the long term will generally lead to lower accumulated investment accounts, over the short term there may be no connection between errors and rate of return realized. An investor decision is judged to be an error if it is based on a faulty decision-making process or on the use of incorrect information or concepts concerning investments. It is not dependent on the investor having suffered a financial loss.

The Employee Retirement Income Security Act of 1974 (ERISA) provides a legal definition of investor error for U.S. employer-managed pension plans. That definition is called the "prudent man" or "prudent expert" rule. In managing a pension plan's assets, an individual must act "with the care, skill, prudence, and diligence under the circumstances then prevailing that a prudent man acting in a like capacity and familiar with such matters would use in conducting an enterprise of like character and with like aims" (ERISA §404[a][1][B]). With this definition, a portfolio's overall performance is judged rather than the performance or choice of particular holdings in isolation.

Pension participant investment errors fall into two broad categories: lack of information and poor information processing (New 1999). Lack of information can include inadequate knowledge of investing or of stock markets, and biased information about stock markets. Poor information processing can be due to faulty logic (Bodie 2003).

Information may be so complex that, even if it is supplied, pension investors are not able to make rational choices (Barr 2001). This failure may occur because the long time horizon for retirement investment decisions makes it difficult for people to understand the consequences of their choices. Investor errors may also result from overconfidence. Males may be more likely to suffer from overconfidence in their ability as investors, possibly because some males believe they have superior knowledge concerning the mathematics and concepts of finance (Barber and Odean 2001).

TYPES OF INVESTOR ERRORS

Pension investor errors resulting from these factors can be categorized under three broad headings: 1) insufficient diversification, 2) inappropriate level of risk holdings in a diversified portfolio, and 3) inappropriate portfolio adjustments.

Insufficient Diversification

Portfolio diversification can only be judged within the context of the entire portfolio of participants or, if married, of their families, including their expected social security and defined benefit pension benefits. Thus, it would be incorrect to view a pension portfolio that is undiversified as necessarily representing a problem, since the pension participant may achieve diversification in other assets that he or she holds. However, for many participants, the pension plan is their major financial investment. In that context, pension participants may make the following investment errors.

Failure to understand the basic principles of diversification

This source of error leads workers to insufficiently diversify between stocks and bonds, and also to insufficiently diversify within the stock portion of the portfolio. Unsophisticated investors may wrongly think that investing in an undiversified, risky portfolio will be rewarded with a commensurately higher expected return. Lucas (2000), examining the portfolios of 250,000 401(k) plan participants, found that, typically, portfolios are poorly diversified, focusing mainly on stable value, large capitalization stock, and company shares issued by the participant's employer.

Participants' portfolios may be poorly diversified by not holding any bonds or by having a relatively small share of their portfolio in bonds. To the extent that investors base their portfolio decisions on their experience, young people who have never known a major decline in the stock market may overinvest in equities relative to bonds. Being well diversified requires holding mutual funds in various asset classes—including foreign stocks, real estate, and bonds—and pension participants may not feel comfortable investing in that many different types of assets. Insufficient diversification has been a common problem in Sweden. Even though the Swedish economy represents less than 1 percent of the world economy, Swedish workers who chose funds invested nearly half of their assets in Swedish equity funds (Thaler 2005).

Dividing by *n*

This error involves dividing the investment portfolio equally among all available investment options (*n* being the number of investment options), which means that, if a pension plan offers three choices, the participant making this error would split his or her contribution in thirds. This practice results in an asset allocation to stocks and bonds that depends on the number and composition of stock and bond funds offered by the sponsoring employer (Benartzi and Thaler 2001). Holden and VanDerhei (2001) explored this pattern and found that only a small percentage of workers appear to manage their pension portfolios this way.

Picking specialized mutual funds rather than broad-based funds

This strategy makes diversification difficult to achieve with a small portfolio. Pension investors may fail to adequately diversify if their plan gives them a large number of fund choices and allows them to pick funds that concentrate on a narrow segment of the market. For many years, the Thrift Savings Plan for federal government employees only allowed federal government workers a choice of three broad funds. In 2001, it added a small cap fund and an international fund. Single-choice portfolios that in one fund offer a broad diversification of stocks and bonds, including international investments, may be desirable because they make it easier for employees to diversify (Quinn 2002).

Picking investments one is familiar with rather than broadly diversifying

This may explain why individuals fail to invest in foreign stocks. However, fees charged in foreign stock funds tend to be higher than in domestic funds, and investors may not have adequate protections in some foreign stock markets.

Too Much or Too Little Diversified Risk

Even participants who understand diversification and have well-diversified portfolios may hold an inappropriate amount of diversified investment risk, given their time horizon and degree of risk aversion.[1] Risk aversion depends on a person's attitude toward risk, but it may also be affected by knowledge. One theory that connects financial knowledge with investment choices is "uncertainty aversion." This theory posits that individuals who think imprecisely about probabilities tend to behave in a more risk-averse manner than those with more precise beliefs (Ellsberg 1961, Lillard and Willis 2001). Lillard and Willis (2001) found that more precise probabilistic thinking by a person was linked to a willingness to take on more risks, and ultimately to a higher growth in wealth. Women are more likely to be averse to uncertainty than men, but their uncertainty aversion may decrease over time as they gain more experience with investments (McCarthy and Turner 2000).

Just as some people prefer chocolate ice cream to vanilla, some people prefer less risk to more risk. From an economic perspective, the preference for chocolate or the preference for risk is not superior to the alternative. A policy issue arises, however, when conservative (overly low-risk) investing is caused by ignorance—that is, by lack of knowledge about financial markets and concepts. It is important to discern why some workers invest conservatively because different reasons have different policy implications.

The government may have a legitimate role in providing financial education when a mandatory individual account requires the participant to make portfolio decisions. Changes in behavior based on increased information are desirable. Investment education provided to pension participants appears to affect pension investment decisions (McCarthy and Turner 2000) and to increase the equity holdings of pension participants in their nonpension portfolios (Weisbenner 1999).

In some aspects of investing, financial advisers do not agree on the appropriate strategy. Many advisers tell clients who are nearing retirement to reduce the amount of risk they hold. Some counselors use a rule of thumb, for example, of subtracting the worker's age from the number 80: the remaining percentage, which declines as the worker ages, is the fraction of his or her wealth that should be invested in the stock market. Others argue that this rule of thumb is too conservative, but that replacing the number 80 with 100 would be satisfactory. An alternative view is that older investors should continue to take risks, investing at age 60 as they did when they were in their 40s (Pollan and Levine 2001). This advice would lead to a higher portfolio share of equities at older ages than would occur under traditional advice.

Another factor that affects risk-bearing is a person's ability and willingness to postpone retirement in the face of adverse portfolio returns. Workers with more flexibility may accept a riskier pension portfolio because they can delay retirement if their assets fall short (Bodie 2001).

Still others base their views as to appropriate pension investments on analysis of the effects of tax law. One recommendation is that participants should invest their pension assets in heavily taxed investment instruments because pension plans are tax exempt. In the United States, this would lead one to invest in taxable bonds because these bonds do not receive the favorable tax treatment enjoyed by unrealized capital gains on stocks (Black 1980). Another analysis based on tax law argues, however, that most individual investors hold mutual funds, and the tax law creates advantages for holding equity mutual funds in the individual account and bond mutual funds outside the individual account (Shoven 1999). The comparison depends on the extent to which dividends are paid and the turnover of shares.

Because an investor's aversion to risk is a factor in investment choice, it is difficult for a financial analyst to determine that a person is holding too much or too little risk. Nonetheless, as we have seen, some investors may make choices out of a poor understanding of the uncertainty of different investments.

The structure of an individual account may induce some workers to take on too much financial market risk. In the Chilean system, there is an incentive for low-income workers to invest in the most speculative mutual funds. If those funds perform well, individuals keep the gains, but if they perform poorly, the workers can claim social assistance benefits (James 2005).

Inappropriate Portfolio Choices and Adjustments

In addition to errors concerning risk and diversification, individual account participants may make poor choices as to the assets in which they invest or the manner in which they adjust or fail to adjust their portfolios. These problems can lead to lower retirement income.

Failure to take fees into account

One source of error in making portfolio choices is to ignore investment fees when deciding among different investments. This mistake is abetted by the investment industry's practice of only disclosing fees in the prospectus and not in other informational materials. Also, educational materials the financial industry provides to pension participants frequently do not list charges as a factor to consider in making portfolio choices.

Expectation-based errors

Naïve expectations as to the stock market's future course are another reason for mistakes. Such expectations can involve the idea that the economy and the stock market have substantially changed so that past experience is of little relevance in terms of future market volatility or the possibility of a sustained downturn. For example, during a prolonged bull market, some participants may believe that economic science has advanced to the point that the risk of a stock market decline has been substantially reduced.

The view as to investor errors based on faulty expectations depends to some extent on the accepted theory of stock market price changes. This theory involves the possibility of overpricing of the stock market and stock market bubbles versus pricing that perfectly reflects current knowledge about factors that affect future profitability. Stock market bubbles occur when prices are bid up to inflated levels and then drop precipitously. A dramatic example of this occurred in Japan, where the Nikkei stock market index rose to over 40,000 and subsequently fell to 10,000. Thus, investor error based on faulty expectations depends on what are "rational" expectations for future stock market prices.

Anticipating that trends will continue may be another source of error. This can be characterized as fear when the market is declining and greed when the market is rising. It can also be seen as erroneous belief in the "law of small numbers": the fallacy that, based on a sample of a limited number of years, trends will continue. Some people may give too much weight to recent experience and extrapolate recent trends that are inconsistent with long-run averages. Expecting that a downward trend will continue may cause some participants to stop investing in equities, losing the advantage of dollar cost averaging, whereby participants always purchase the same dollar value of stocks, with more stocks being purchased when the price is low than when it is high. Participants may become discouraged when the stock market falls and sell at low points, perhaps expecting further erosion. For example, in July 2002, after a period of stock market declines, the Hewitt 401(k) Index found that participants had a tendency to sell stock funds (Benefitnews.com 2002). Expectations may be falsely based on herding behavior, where investors follow what they think other people are doing.

The opposite error is to believe that, because stock prices have fallen, it is a good time to buy equities. This approach is encapsulated in the folk wisdom that a stock market decline means that the market is having a "sale."

The error of following trends at a lag results in buying high and selling low. This occurs when investors shift their investments to the sector performing best at the time. For example, investors may switch out of stocks into bonds, or out of growth stocks into value stocks during a market downturn. In Sweden, among workers making an active choice, the most commonly chosen fund in 2000 was a Swedish technology fund that had risen 534 percent in the five preceding years, but then lost 70 percent in the following three years (Thaler 2005).

Picking actively traded mutual funds that have outperformed the market, expecting that they will continue to do so, is also an error. Past performance does not predict future results, and, in fact, past winners tend to underperform the market (Baer and Gensler 2002).

Errors due to inertia

Investor errors may occur because of inertia or from faulty views about one's own abilities as an investor. Some people tend to be affected by inertia and fail to revise their initial investment allocation when their pension plan starts to offer further options, or they fail to make other adjustments to their portfolios. One study found that most pension participants in TIAA-CREF made no adjustments to their asset allocation over their entire career (Samuelson and Zeckhauser 1988). Another study found that nearly half of TIAA-CREF participants made no changes over a 10-year period (Ameriks and Zeldes 2004). (TIAA-CREF is a national pension system for employees of educational and research institutions.) The effects of inertia can be overcome by investing in a lifestyle fund that adjusts its portfolio according to the age of the participant.

Participants' failing to rebalance their portfolios after a run of stock price increases or decreases may be a manifestation of inertia. Lucas (2000) found that pension participants do not adjust their portfolios to their time horizon. Portfolios tend to have similar risk levels across age groups from 25 to 50. Equity exposure only decreases materially for the portfolio of the typical participant at age 60 or older. Lucas suggests that automatic rebalancing of a participant's initial choice of asset allocation may be a desirable way to deal with this issue.

Policy Implications

This discussion suggests a number of policies for controlling participants' investments that could minimize the common errors made by individual pension investors:

- Do not permit participants to invest in individual stocks.
- Do not allow participants to invest in mutual funds with a narrow market focus.
- Do not permit participants to invest an entire pension account in highly risky investments such as high-tech stocks.
- Encourage participants to put the majority of investments in passively managed funds.
- Advise participants to consider investment fees when choosing an investment.
- Educate employees on common investment mistakes participants make.
- Limit the number of investment choices. Too many choices may cause more workers to take the default option because they are overwhelmed by the number of options.
- Carefully consider the portfolio of the default fund so that that fund will offer a good choice for most workers.
- Present the default fund as being a good choice for workers not wanting to or able to choose a fund.
- Encourage the development of single-choice funds that are diversified across asset classes, that automatically rebalance, and that reduce their risk exposure as the participant approaches retirement.

WOMEN AND PENSION INVESTMENTS

Are individual accounts good for women? An individual account is often a worker's largest investment in financial markets. The shift toward retirement sources that involve portfolio decisions by workers has important implications for the adequacy of retirement income for women. Evidence suggests that women are generally more conservative investors than men and are less knowledgeable about financial principles. Because of more cautious investing, women's choices may contribute to the persistence of a gender-related "pension gap." Lower-risk investments have a lower expected return, causing investments by women to result in less retirement income than for men who contribute the same amount to their individual accounts. Empirical evidence indicates that, on average, women hold lower amounts of risk in pension portfolios than do men.

Women, Men, and Risk-Bearing in Pension Investments

The shift of investment fund management from professionals to pension participants allows individuals to choose portfolios suited to their needs and to their attitudes toward risk. Some people, particularly women, however, may be overly conservative, allocating too large a percentage of their pension fund account balance to bonds.

Women, men, and risk aversion

Women are generally less prone to take risks than men, even when income, wealth, and other socioeconomic factors are taken into account. For example, women are less likely to engage in risky behaviors such as skydiving, drinking and driving, and smoking (Bajtelsmit and Bernasek 1996; Barber and Odean 2001).

Examining risk preference questions in the Survey of Consumer Finances, Jianakoplos (1999) found that 42 percent of women stated an unwillingness to take any financial risks, compared to 29 percent of men. At the other extreme, 2.9 percent of women indicated a willingness to take substantial financial risk, versus 4.4 percent of men. Interestingly, Jianakoplos found that women's stated risk preferences often contradicted observed investment patterns. Of the women who reported that they were willing to take the most financial risks, 46 percent held only risk-free assets, compared to only 1 percent of the men stating that risk tolerance. Equally surprising, households that stated an unwillingness to take any financial risks were found to have 35 percent of their total assets in risky investments. Jianakoplos concludes that stated risk preferences provide an ordinal ranking of observed investment patterns, but that they are a poor predictor of quantitative ranking.

Gender differences in wealth and income

While male-female differences in risk aversion have often been viewed as the cause of variations in investments among workers with similar characteristics, recent research has attempted to provide explanations that do not rely on differences in attitudes toward risk. Gender differences in wealth and income are one such explanation. Other possible reasons include differences in investment knowledge, in precision concerning thinking about probabilities, and in confidence about one's financial knowledge.

Studies have found that gender differences in investment choices diminish or even disappear as income rises. These results may reflect the fact that women with high incomes are better situated to bear financial market risk than women with low incomes, or that they are more likely to have private pension income and other accumulated savings than are low- or moderate-income women. Another possibility is that income is correlated with education and, by extension, with financial knowledge. Finally, women with higher incomes may have longer experience in managing their own savings.

Hinz, McCarthy, and Turner (1996) analyzed how much of the gender differential in risk-bearing could be explained by economic and demographic attributes of the workers in their sample. Using data from a 1990 survey of participants in the federal government's Thrift Savings Plan for its employees, the authors examined the effects of salary, other family income, age, and marital status. During the survey year, federal government workers had the option to invest their pension money in three funds: stocks, government bonds, and a fixed-income fund of both government and corporate bonds. The authors found that 45 percent of men, but only 28 percent of women, placed any money in the stock fund. A large percentage of the sample, 65 percent of women and 52 percent of men, invested only in the minimum-risk government bond fund.[2] At the other end of the risk spectrum, 11 percent of men and 5 percent of women invested the maximum allowable percentage (60 percent of their own contributions) in the common stock fund. The analysis also showed that higher earners of both genders were significantly more likely than lower earners to contribute to the common stock fund; in this regard, the effect of one's own salary was 10 times greater than that of other family income. The gender gap did not disappear with rising income, however: holding constant the worker's salary and other family income, men were still more likely to invest in the common stock and fixed-income funds than were women. Additional studies have also found that women were more likely to invest in fixed-income securities and less likely to put money in stock than men, even controlling for other economic and demographic characteristics of workers (Bajtelsmit and VanDerhei 1996; Agnew, Balduzzi, and Sundén 2000; Muller 2000). These studies imply that in an individual account system, women's conservative investments would tend to exacerbate the existing gender pension gap.

A prominent study that points in another direction found that in pension plans that included the choice of company stock, women held a greater proportion of their portfolios in fixed-income assets than men but a smaller portfolio share of the company stock than men (Clark et al. 1996). The picture changed dramatically for pension plans that did not offer company stock. In such plans, women at all income levels generally held a higher percentage of their portfolios in equities than did men, with the exception of young men at the low and high tails of the earnings distribution.

Financial knowledge, precise thinking about risk, and confidence

McCarthy and Turner (2000) studied the determinants of workers' self-assessment of their financial sophistication and noted a large gender difference. (Self-assessment was done simply by having workers rate their own level of knowledge.) Males, older workers, and higher-income workers had greater self-assessed financial knowledge. A typical man's assessment of his own financial knowledge was equivalent to the self-assessed financial knowledge of an otherwise similar woman 23 years older. McCarthy and Turner also found that workers with a higher self-assessment of their financial knowledge selected riskier investments and thus had portfolios with a higher expected rate of return. This study suggests that part of the gender difference in pension risk-bearing that is unexplained in other studies could be due to a differential in financial knowledge.

Differences in self-assessed financial knowledge between the genders may also reflect, in part, overconfidence by male investors. Barber and Odean (2001) define overconfident investors as those who ultimately lower their returns because their belief in their own knowledge about securities exceeds their actual knowledge. Overconfident investors trade excessively and hold portfolios that are riskier than the portfolios held by rational investors with the same degree of risk aversion. Barber and Odean's study of trading at a discount brokerage firm found that single men traded 67 percent more than single women, thereby lowering their returns net of trading costs by 1.44 percentage points per year compared to single women.

Muller (2000) studied the effects of taking a retirement class on workers' asset allocation, using the Health and Retirement Survey (HRS) data. She found that for those with a high level of risk aversion, retirement education substantially increased the percentage they invested in equities. Retirement education had no effect, however, on the equity choices made by other groups of participants.

Pension investment experience also may affect the financial choices that participants make outside their pension plans. Bajtelsmit and Jianakoplos (2001) found that households with individual accounts that offered investment choice were 5 percent more likely to hold stock outside their pensions than were households without individual accounts. They ascribe this finding to the theory that participation in an individual account lowers the deterrents to stock ownership that may exist because of unfamiliarity.

Household decision-making and investment

The discussion thus far has assumed that married individuals make financial decisions without consulting their spouse. An added dimension in pension investment and other financial decisions of men and women is how such choices are made within families.

One hypothesis is that marriage provides insurance through income pooling, with the employment of husbands and wives when both work outside the home generally being subject to different risks. Consequently, married couples might take greater investment risks even after holding constant family income. The analysis is complicated, however, by the fact that married people are more likely to have dependents. Moreover, married couples have longer life expectancies than single individuals. The direction of these combined effects on pension investments is unclear.

As a result of spousal consultation, it might be expected that gender differences in risk-bearing in individual accounts would be muted for married workers. The extent to which spouses made financial decisions independently or as a couple was explored by Elder (1999), using the first wave of the Health and Retirement Survey. Participants in this study were between the ages of 51 and 61 in 1991. Their partners, who were also surveyed, included some younger and older individuals. Elder found that 40 percent of couples agreed that financial decisions were made equally in their household. The phrasing of the survey response, "we equally make the decision," unfortunately does not shed much light on whether respondents took "equally" to mean that the spouses coordinated their financial decisions, or that each partner made separate choices concerning his or her own assets. Thirty-six percent of couples disagreed on which party made financial decisions. Older and white respondents were more likely to believe that the other individual made the financial decisions, or that these were made jointly.

Hinz, McCarthy, and Turner (1996) found that marriage had a significantly negative effect on a participant's stock investment in a pension plan: marriage tended to make both men and women less likely to invest in either stock or a fixed-income bond fund that included both government and corporate bonds. Married men and unmarried women tended to take similar risks. Married women were the most cautious, while unmarried men had the least conservative investments. One possible interpretation is that the combined husband-wife portfolio is intermediate in risk between the portfolios of the two people acting as single individuals.

PSYCHOLOGICAL EFFECTS OF INDIVIDUAL ACCOUNTS ON PARTICIPANTS

Although human behavior affects the functioning of individual accounts, the reverse may also occur. In the debate over the use of mandatory individual accounts for social security reform, a number of psychological effects on participants of having mandatory individual accounts have been posited.

The sanctity of the ownership rights to private property is a fundamental aspect of American political psychology (Lerner 1957). An issue raised by those who favor individual accounts is that people would feel as if they own these assets: the account balance would be clear, and the government could not take actions that would reduce its value (Box 5.2). They also posit that people do not feel ownership of their Social Security benefit, in part because it could be diminished by future legislation. The U.S. Supreme Court ruling in *Flemming v. Nestor* (63 U.S. 603 [1960]), frequently cited by policy analysts who favor individual accounts as part of Social Security, stated that workers and beneficiaries have no legal ownership of their Social Security benefits (Cogan and Mitchell 2003).

Related to the feeling of ownership is that of control. People have some control over the investment of their individual account balance, while they have none over their Social Security benefit. Individual control is often cited by voters as the main reason for favoring individual accounts, even over higher benefits or the ability to pass on the account to their heirs (Biggs 2002).

The President's Commission (2001) argued that there were a number of psychological benefits to workers holding assets in individual accounts. The commission said that asset holding has a substantial positive effect on long-term health and marital stability, even when control-

---

Box 5.2 Individual Accounts and Ownership

Individual accounts have been favored by some people as extending ownership rights in U.S. society. However, the ownership rights to individual accounts differ greatly between add-on accounts and carve-out accounts. With an add-on individual account, the individual has ownership rights with no offsets against those rights. That is not the case with carve-out accounts. Carve-out accounts are more like a loan than like outright ownership. When a worker takes a carve-out account, the government in effect gives the worker a loan. The loan is the reduction in Social Security tax payments, which the worker uses to contribute to the individual account. At retirement, the worker pays back the loan through a reduction in Social Security benefits. Thus, the worker does not own the voluntary carve-out individual account in the same way that an add-on account is owned, because he or she must pay back the loan that was used to create the carve-out account.

ling for income, race, and education. In addition, saving patterns are passed on from parents to children. Parents who save are more likely to have children who save.

In Chile, some have argued that having funded individual accounts has turned workers into capitalists in their way of thinking. Participants are less likely to support government economic policies that are adverse to capital. Consequently, according to the rationale, this has caused workers to be more attached to the free market and to a free society. This in turn has reduced the traditional conflicts between workers and owners of capital. It has depoliticized the Chilean economy and promoted political stability. Pensions are no longer an issue for political demagoguery (Rodriguez 2001).

As a presumed consequence, Chile is the first South American nation to sign a free trade agreement with the United States. It is argued that Chilean workers support free trade policies because of their capital market holdings through their pension accounts. While trade liberalization and globalization are often cast as a battle between capitalists and workers, Chilean workers consider an anticapitalist to be both anticapital and antiworker (Piñera 2003). In the United States, some have argued that holding stocks in pension funds has made workers less likely to support other employees in collective bargaining disagreements.

CONCLUSIONS

Individual accounts as part of social security generally rely on the participant to make investment decisions. Many low-income and less-educated people have no experience or knowledge in managing investments. Some do not even have bank accounts. Even high-income and well-educated workers make predictable mistakes in financial management. Experience with individual accounts as part of social security in Sweden indicates that many employees do not make an investment choice, and thus the structure of the default fund is an important aspect of the system design.

This chapter has discussed a number of factors that influence investment decisions by individuals and that may result in poor choices: pension portfolios may be inadequately diversified or not reflective of an asset strategy appropriate to the age of the participant. One's level of education, income, gender, and marital status underlie differences in investment approaches, which will result in differences in levels of retirement income.

Financial education may be an important aspect of an individual account system. A policy issue arises to the extent that conservative investing is caused by ignorance—that is, by lack of knowledge about financial markets and concepts. Thus, it is important to discern why some workers invest conservatively, because different reasons have different policy implications. Employers and the government may have a legitimate role in providing financial education when the pension plan they sponsor requires participants to make portfolio decisions. Changes in behavior based on increased information are desirable. There is evidence that investment education provided to pension participants affects pension investment decisions and that it increases the equity holdings of participants in their nonpension portfolios.

Notes

1. A leading scholar in the field writes, "There is currently no consensus on the optimal asset allocation strategy for investors..." (Poterba 2001).
2. One possible explanation for the high rate of government bond ownership among both genders is that the Thrift Savings Plan statute required, in 1987, that all employee contributions be invested in the government bond fund. This requirement decreased every year by 20 percent and was eliminated in 1991. Thus, some employees may not have moved out of the bond fund because of inertia. The authors investigated this hypothesis in a separate regression by entering a variable for participation in the plan in 1987, but the variable was not statistically significant.

6
Labor Market Issues

It is often argued that, while defined benefit pension plans distort the labor market decisions of workers, reducing their hours of work, individual accounts are nondistortionary and thus would result in greater work by participants (World Bank 1994). Voluntary individual accounts can be designed to affect neither the actions of employees and employers nor the distribution of income. However, the presumption that individual accounts are nondistortionary is considerably stronger for voluntary than for mandatory plans. With voluntary plans, people may choose not to take them, while, with mandatory plans, workers may view the contributions as a tax.

An examination of the actual features of mandated individual accounts indicates that those plans generally do affect retirement and job choice (Turner 2000). Any mandatory program that attempts to increase people's retirement savings may change their labor supply behavior, as discussed in the following sections. This impact occurs because individuals act to minimize the program's effects and because of the effects of the worker's greater retirement savings, if the program succeeds in that regard.

EFFECTS ON HOURS WORKED

A mandatory individual account may affect hours worked if employees view the mandatory contributions as a tax rather than as being equivalent to voluntary savings (Burkhauser and Turner 1985). How people view the contributions depends on their expectations as to future benefits derived from those contributions. If they mistrust the system and are skeptical that they will receive commensurate benefits in return, they will tend to view the payments they make as a tax (Box 6.1).

A mandatory contribution rate that is greater than what a worker would voluntarily pay may be viewed as a tax by individuals who can-

Box 6.1   The Distorting Effect of Taxes

Taxes distort the labor supply decisions of workers by reducing the monetary returns from work, and thus the incentive to work and presumably the amount of work done. Some economists have argued that switching from Social Security to carve-out individual accounts would increase the amount of work done in the United States by reducing the distorting effect of taxes. This argument is based on workers viewing the Social Security payroll tax as a tax for which they receive little or nothing in return. While the amount of government services a person receives has little direct connection to the income taxes he or she pays, that is not the case for Social Security. As indicated by the annual statement workers receive from the Social Security Administration, the more they pay in Social Security payroll taxes, the higher will be their benefits. Because of the progressive redistribution within Social Security, for some workers Social Security may act as a wage subsidy rather than as a tax.

not borrow at low rates to restore their consumption to the level desired. The higher that required contributions rise above what a worker would want to pay, the more likely the person will perceive the amounts as a tax. (See Appendix B at the end of this book.) To the extent that this occurs, the contributions would have the normal wealth and substitution effects associated with taxes and would presumably reduce hours worked. These effects of mandatory individual accounts (discussed in the next section) would probably not be relevant for voluntary carve-out accounts because the total amount contributed to social security would be the same.

Coronado (1997) has attempted to estimate whether workers perceive required contributions as a tax in the Chilean mandatory individual account system. She finds that, under the individual account system, the mandatory contributions were viewed as less of a tax than under the former pay-as-you-go system. However, she is unable to rule out that participants see some of the contributions under the mandatory individual account system as a tax.

Individual accounts may affect hours worked by older persons because of the flexibility of such plans. These accounts may facilitate a phased reduction in work hours preceding retirement. For example, Sweden's mandatory individual account system permits workers to take one-quarter, one-half, three-quarters, or full benefits. By taking partial benefits, a worker could finance a phased reduction in work hours. Workers are eligible to take either partial or full benefits at age 61. Defined benefit plans can be designed with this feature, but it is more complex to do so.

EFFECTS ON RETIREMENT AGE

While it is generally thought that mandatory individual accounts do not affect the age at which workers retire, that may not be the case. Aspects of individual accounts that may affect the worker's retirement age include the following: interaction with other programs, the current interest rate used for annuitizing the account balance versus anticipated interest rates, the extent to which past rates of return on the account balance have been unexpected, expected future rates of return, the riskiness associated with expected future rates of return, requirements as to the age at which benefits can or must be taken, rules as to whether work must cease when drawing benefits, and the level of the mandatory contribution rate. The effects of individual accounts on retirement age can be divided into those effects that relate to the accumulation of account balances and those that relate to the way in which benefits are paid.

Account Balances

Account balances can affect the timing of retirement in several ways. First, there may be wealth effects associated with mandatory individual accounts or voluntary carve-out accounts. If individual accounts have received unexpectedly favorable rates of return, positive wealth effects may induce workers to retire (Diamond 1998). The reverse would be the case if the rates of return had been lower than anticipated.

Hermes and Ghilarducci (2006) present evidence for the United States suggesting that negative wealth effects from the decline in stock

markets in the early 2000s caused some pension participants to postpone retirement. They argue that this effect of individual accounts de-
stabilizes labor markets because workers are encouraged to postpone
retirement at the time when the economy is doing poorly and firms are
likely to be laying off workers. As a result, firms have greater difficulty
adjusting to economic fluctuations, and workers seeking employment
have a harder time securing a job.

Second, there may be a substitution effect related to anticipated
rates of return on the assets held in the pension plan. The substitution
effect can be thought of as the option value of delaying retirement and
contributing to an individual account for another year. This effect would
lead to postponed retirement if the worker expected to receive a relatively high rate of return on the pension fund balance or on pension contributions that depend on continued employment (Disney, Palacios, and
Whitehouse 1999). For example, employees might be induced to delay
retirement if they were forced to annuitize their account balances at
retirement but felt they could receive a better rate of return on pension
investments if they continued working and thus were able to continue
investing their account balance.

Third, the higher the contribution rates and the more money accumulated in the plan, the more likely is the plan to affect retirement if
the worker is liquidity-constrained. Being unable to borrow against his
account balance to finance current consumption, the worker would need
to retire to gain access to the cash in his pension account.

The Chilean pension system has a feature that allows people in
physically demanding occupations to retire earlier than other workers.
In those occupations, the employer must contribute an additional 2 percent of wages to each individual's pension account. Economic theory
suggests that workers would bear those added costs through reduced
wages. The extra payment permits workers to accumulate sufficient account balances to retire earlier than they otherwise would be able to.

Fourth, the riskiness of the plan's investments will affect the degree
of certainty that individuals attach to their intended retirement age. The
riskier the plan, the more uncertain workers will be as to their likely
account balances at the age at which they expect to retire. The effect of
riskiness of the asset returns on retirement age may depend on workers'
attitudes toward risk-taking (Kingston 2000). Financially conservative
persons, when the perceived risk-return trade-off improves, will tend to

stop working earlier: retirement has become cheaper to finance in terms of the risk that must be borne. However, workers who tolerate more risk will postpone retirement: by taking the same amount of risk, they will receive higher returns, which will allow greater future consumption.

Finally, the early retirement age in social security may play an important psychological role, acting as a signal of the age at which the government considers it reasonable for people to retire. Thus, the age at which workers can begin receiving benefits from individual accounts may send a message that could cause people to retire earlier or later than otherwise.

Benefit Receipt

Several aspects of benefit receipt may affect when workers retire. One factor may be the extent to which individual accounts pay benefits as a lump sum. At least two aspects of uncertainty are associated with whether a lump sum will provide adequate retirement income. First, length of life is unknown. Second, there is unpredictability as to the future value of the lump sum because of fluctuations in market rates of return. These factors may induce workers, who are concerned that they not run out of money, to postpone their retirement age from the age at which they would choose to retire in a plan providing an annuitized benefit of equal expected value (Munnell, Cahill, and Jivan 2003). However, if lump sum benefits are available at an earlier age than are annuitized benefits, myopic workers may take the lump sum benefits.

Individual accounts may affect retirement age because of their interactions with other government programs. For example, by retiring at the earliest possible age with nonannuitized benefits, low-income workers in Chile may be able to qualify later for government-subsidized minimum benefits after they have spent down their pension assets. A similar strategy may be used by Australian low-income workers in order to receive increased means-tested benefits at a later age. Australia's individual account system suffers from an incentive for workers to retire early and rely on the government pension once they are eligible. By taking early retirement, workers reduce the pension benefit that is based on their own contributions and receive a larger benefit from the income-tested and asset-tested age pension.

If workers are unable to borrow against their individual accounts, which is generally the case when individual accounts are part of social security, and they are otherwise liquidity-constrained, they may be induced to retire, as that would be the only way to access their funds. However, if people cannot withdraw funds from their account before a certain age, or cannot withdraw them before a certain age without tax penalty, or cannot withdraw them before other criteria are met (such as a minimum replacement rate provided by the account), workers may be induced to postpone retirement until they meet the necessary requirements.

If the account balance is annuitized, individual accounts, either mandatory or voluntary carve-out, may affect workers' retirement decisions because of the effect of changes in the interest rate on the level of monthly benefits provided by an annuity. The lower the interest rate, the lower the monthly benefit resulting from converting the account balance to an annuity. Workers with individual accounts may retire early or postpone retirement based on how favorably they view the interest rate in the annuity market compared to their expectations for future rates. This effect would not be considered to distort behavior since it is a reaction to market prices rather than to the effect of taxes distorting prices.

Fluctuations in annuity rates and in financial markets may have large combined effects on the level of retirement benefits provided by individual accounts, and thus on retirement age. Workers retiring in the United States in 1969 who had a pension plan invested entirely in stock over their career and who annuitized their benefit would have received a pension equal to 100 percent of their final preretirement earnings; in contrast, because of the stock market downturn, workers retiring six years later, in 1975, would have received a pension benefit providing a 42 percent replacement rate (Burtless 2000a).

One study, using the Health and Retirement Survey, tested empirically for the effect of individual accounts on the age at which workers retire in the United States (Friedberg and Webb 2000). The finding was that, for workers who have both a defined benefit and an individual account, the greater the balance in the individual account, the greater the probability of retirement in a given period. Given that effect, it was unexpected that the authors did not see an influence of account balance on retirement age for workers having only an individual account. Another study found that U.S. workers whose employer provides only an individual account plan tended to retire a year later than similar workers whose employer provides only a defined benefit plan (Munnell, Cahill, and Jivan 2003).

Changes in Retirement Eligibility Age in Individual Accounts

With gains in longevity, a given account balance at a fixed retirement age provides lower annual benefits for each successive birth cohort. Perhaps for this reason, some mandatory individual account systems have raised the earliest age at which benefits can be received.

The choice of the earliest age at which benefits can be received is an important aspect of plan design. Some empirical work suggests that about a third of the U.S. population has a high time preference rate, which implies that they will take social security benefits at the earliest age at which they are available (Gustman and Steinmeier 2005). Because these workers may take benefits at an early age if they are available, with the result being that they receive a low level of benefits, the age at which benefits are available will affect the age at which workers actually retire. The following examples tell of countries that have raised the eligibility age at which individual account benefits can be received.

Australia

For both men and women born before July 1, 1960, the minimum age at which the mandatory superannuation benefit (the Australian terminology for the mandatory individual account) can be received is 55. That age has been raised (as of 1999) for later birth cohorts, affecting those aged 38 and younger at the time of the change. For those born after July 1, 1960, but before July 1, 1961, the minimum age is 56. In similar fashion, the minimum age rises by one year for every subsequent birth cohort until it reaches age 60 for those born after June 30, 1964 (Kehl 2002).

Chile

In Chile, workers may begin drawing their pension benefits at any age so long as their benefits are at least 110 percent of the legal minimum wage, which is a minimum benefit guaranteed to all workers who have contributed for 20 years, and at least 50 percent of their own average wage. These requirements will be raised to 150 percent and 70 percent, respectively, by 2010 (James, Martinez, and Iglesias 2004). This arrangement provides flexibility for workers, yet it is intended to ensure that people will not retire at an early age with insufficient benefits.

Sweden

When Sweden reformed its retirement income system in 1999 and introduced the mandatory defined contribution Premium Pension system, it raised the early retirement age in 2000 from 60 to 61 (SSA 1999).

CONCLUSIONS

This chapter has explored various possible effects of mandatory individual accounts and voluntary carve-out accounts on workers in labor markets. In some instances, effects depend on whether the account is mandatory or voluntary, while in other cases, the same results would be expected for either one. The hypotheses discussed here in regard to how individual accounts may affect labor supply and demand await further analytical development and empirical testing.

An important aspect of the labor market effects of individual accounts depends on whether workers view mandatory contributions as being a tax or as being savings. The higher the mandatory contribution and the greater the extent to which workers are myopic or lack confidence in the system (thus placing little value on future benefits), the more likely they are to see it as a tax (see Appendix B).

Individual accounts may have wealth as well as substitution effects. Wealth effects due to capital market changes may influence workers' decisions as to when to retire. This consequence may be destabilizing on labor markets because workers are induced to postpone retirement during periods of economic downturn, at the same time that firms are laying off personnel. Individual accounts may affect the age of retirement for some low-income workers because of the way those plans interact with poverty programs in certain countries.

A related issue is the effect of gains in longevity on the age at which workers are eligible to receive benefits from individual accounts. As life expectancy improves, either the contribution rate must increase or the age of early retirement must be raised in order to keep constant the benefits provided by individual accounts. Some countries have raised the earliest age at which individual account benefits can be received, which can be considered as containing an aspect of political risk.

7
Benefits and Taxes

Individual accounts accrue in the form of an account balance, but retirees need to receive a steady flow of income to finance their consumption over a number of years. Thus, a decision must be made as to how the account will be converted to an income stream for the retiree—the form in which benefits will be paid. In establishing individual accounts, difficult issues arise concerning payout options and whether, for example, participants should be required to fully annuitize their individual account balances. Public policy also must determine the qualifying conditions for receiving benefits. The structure of pension benefits and the taxation of pensions are closely related—the tax treatment of benefits can have an important effect on the form in which benefits are paid and the amount of benefits received. This chapter also discusses the accrual of benefits.

Pension participants in individual accounts face interest rate risk at the point of retirement if they wish to annuitize their account balances. In defined benefit plans, the plan sponsor bears that risk; the risk is nearly always borne by participants in individual accounts.

To provide examples of ways benefits are paid from individual accounts, the chapter first discusses forms of benefit payment in Sweden and Chile. It then discusses various issues in the determination and payment of benefits. The chapter concludes with a discussion of the tax treatment of individual accounts.

BENEFITS IN THE SWEDISH PREMIUM PENSION SYSTEM

The mandatory individual account system in Sweden, called the Premium Pension system, allows participants considerable flexibility as to when they can begin to receive benefits. Individuals must file a separate claim for the benefit from the notional account plan that provides the majority of social security benefits in Sweden, and for the additional benefit from the Premium Pension (PPM 2003).[1]

Individuals can claim benefits from the mandatory individual account Premium Pension at age 61. There is no maximum age by which benefits must be claimed. Countries often set age limits for workers to start receiving benefits from individual accounts to ensure that the benefits are claimed for retirement purposes, rather than used by high-income earners as a tax-advantaged way to accumulate inheritable wealth. A worker can claim benefits at the same age as he or she initiates benefits from the notional account plan, or that worker can claim benefits from the Premium Pension separately, starting at a different age.

Facilitating semiretirement by permitting partial receipt of benefits, the program allows workers to claim one-quarter, one-half, three-quarters, or full benefits. They can continue working while they draw benefits, in which case they would still contribute to the system (Palmer 2001).

Flexibility for workers as to when they start receiving benefits can be important for reducing the interest rate risk associated with benefit annuitization. However, this flexibility may be of little consequence for older workers who are forced to retire because of ill health or because of losing a job. Interest rate risk in Sweden is limited by a guarantee. The interest rate used to determine the annuity varies with the market, but with a promised minimum of 3 percent. The guarantee is given by the PPM as part of its provision of annuities.

When interest rates are low, the annuity resulting from a given account balance is also relatively low, because the expected income generated from the account is low. A worker can begin receiving benefits from the notional account plan, but if the individual believes interest rates will rise, making it more favorable to annuitize Premium Pension benefits later, the worker can postpone annuitization of the Premium Pension. Once participants have claimed Premium Pension benefits, they can suspend payment or change the percentage of a full payment they receive.

The PPM, the government agency that oversees the Swedish system, is the sole provider of annuities for participants in the Premium Pension. Sweden is the only country where the government is the sole provider of annuities for participants in mandatory individual accounts (World Bank 2000). Typically, in individual accounts, workers who desire to annuitize their account balances must purchase annuities on their own from private-sector life insurance companies.

Although Sweden allows considerable flexibility as to the timing of the initial receipt of benefits, it mandates that, starting from the date the worker first claims Premium Pension benefits, the account balance in the Premium Pension be paid out fully as an annuity. Participants cannot take lump sum payments of even a portion of their account; thus, once they begin collecting benefits, they cannot bequeath any of their account balance.

Participants can choose a fixed or variable annuity. If the person selects a fixed annuity, the PPM guarantees a set monthly payment for life. The monthly amount may be increased by a bonus, however, depending on the PPM's investment experience. If a worker chooses a variable annuity, the Premium Pension benefit may change, because the worker's benefit will be affected by the value of the underlying funds. Benefits workers receive from the Premium Pension are taxable under the personal income tax at the same rate as labor earnings.

The PPM uses unisex life tables, and it uses different life tables for each birth cohort. Because women and higher-wage workers have, on average, longer life expectancies than men and lower-wage workers, the system redistributes money in a complex way from men to women and from lower-wage to higher-wage workers. Consequently, the criticism that traditional defined benefit social security programs redistribute income in a complicated manner also applies to individual accounts that mandate annuitization.

Married workers are not required to provide survivors benefits for their spouses. Participants may voluntarily choose the Premium Pension's survivor benefit, which is primarily used as protection for widows. It is available on a separate basis for the preretirement and retirement periods. Preretirement, participants pay the cost of purchasing a survivor benefit from the funds in the individual worker's account, so it is only available to workers with a sufficient balance to cover the cost of buying the option. This choice first became available in 2005, five years after the start of the system. If the participant elects a survivor benefit and then dies before retirement, the benefit pays a fixed amount (without regard to the participant's account balance) for five years (PPM 2001). Beneficiaries include children under age 20 and a spouse, registered partner, or cohabitant, including same-sex partners.

If the individual at retirement has selected the survivor benefit option, he or she will receive a reduced benefit, and the survivor benefit will be paid as a life annuity to the spouse, registered partner, or person previously married to the deceased or with whom the deceased had children. Workers can also transfer benefits to their spouse or partner by electing to have the contributions they make while working deposited into that person's account instead of their own.

In some individual account systems, the possibility of accumulating bequeathable wealth is considered to be a desirable feature. This opportunity allows lower-income workers to amass funds that they might pass on to their heirs. If a worker dies before having annuitized his or her account balance, the Swedish pension system does not permit the bequest of the remaining sum. That amount is redistributed among all of the participants in the system. A survivors benefit would only be provided if the worker has purchased one.

BENEFITS IN THE CHILEAN PENSION SYSTEM

In Chile, women may claim old-age pension benefits at age 60, and men may claim benefits at age 65. However, the system is flexible in that it allows workers to take benefits at younger ages if they have saved enough in their individual accounts to qualify. They must have sufficient savings so that the annuitized benefit would be at least 50 percent of their average indexed earnings over the previous 10 years, or at least 110 percent of the legal minimum wage, whichever is lower. Workers who have satisfied these requirements can stop contributing and begin withdrawing their money. They need not stop working to collect benefits. This feature allows workers to take partial retirement or phased retirement and to combine employment with the receipt of pension benefits.

Workers may take their benefit as a price-indexed annuity, as a phased withdrawal, or as a combination of the two. With a phased withdrawal, the funds that remain at death become part of the worker's estate. Participants may also take out a lump sum benefit from their individual accounts if the remaining amount is sufficient so that they meet one of two conditions: they purchase an annuity at least equal to 120 percent of the minimum guaranteed pension, or they take scheduled withdrawals of at least 70 percent of the participant's price-indexed covered wages.

The option of a price-indexed annuity in the Chilean system is an unusual feature. While price indexation of benefits occurs frequently in social security defined benefit systems, in individual account systems it is uncommon because most countries do not have price-indexed assets in which to invest to fund price-indexed benefits. Chile, however, has a well-developed market in price-indexed bonds.

With phased withdrawal, the worker receives a benefit each year that is based on his or her remaining life expectancy and on the amount in the person's individual account. With the phased withdrawal, the retirement benefit is recomputed each year, taking into consideration the fund's investment performance and whether the worker's spouse or other beneficiaries have died. Thus, the benefit provided with phased withdrawal differs each year. Pensioners may begin taking their benefits as a phased withdrawal and later switch to a price-indexed annuity.

Chilean pension fund management companies (AFPs) do not provide annuities. At retirement, the participants who choose an annuity must contract with a private insurance company to purchase it. If a married man chooses an annuity, he must provide a survivors annuity for his spouse and minor children. A married woman must do so only if her husband is disabled.

ACCRUAL PATTERN OF BENEFITS
IN INDIVIDUAL ACCOUNTS

The accrual pattern in individual accounts determines how much a worker is gaining in future benefits. This pattern depends on four factors: the worker's age, the worker's earnings, the rate of return, and the accumulated account balance. The earnings of younger people have a larger effect on ultimate account balances than would the same level of earnings at an older age because of interest compounding (Box 7.1).

The time pattern of rates of return can have a large effect on individual accounts. A negative rate of return on a small account early in life has a much smaller effect on balances at retirement than a negative rate of return on a large account near retirement. Thus, different cohorts of workers will receive differing generosity of benefits depending on the

---

**Box 7.1 Unemployment and
Individual Account Accumulations**

For a full-career worker in the United States, a period of unemployment may have little effect on Social Security benefits because those benefits are based on the 35 highest years of earnings, with low-earnings years not being counted for work beyond 35 years. However, with an individual account, any period of unemployment reduces future benefits because it reduces contributions to the account. Because lower-income workers are more likely to become unemployed than higher-income workers, unemployment has more of an effect on retirement income for lower-income workers than for higher-income workers in an individual account system. A less obvious effect is connected with the timing of unemployment relative to the ups and downs of the stock market. If unemployment occurs during market downturns, then unemployed workers are not able to purchase stock when its price is low. Thus, the timing of unemployment affects the amount of lost retirement income. One study (Seligman and Wenger 2005) has found that the actual timing of unemployment tends to make the losses to participants in individual accounts greater than if the timing had been purely random.

---

pattern of high and low rates of return over their working lives, which raises the issue of intergenerational equity.

Making contributions to an individual account nearly always requires that the individual is working. However, the Swedish mandatory individual accounts require that persons who receive unemployment, disability, or child-rearing benefits contribute a part of these benefits to their individual account.

REGRESSIVITY

Retirement income systems may affect the distribution of income among the older population. In some countries, the citizenry has a strong desire to use the retirement income system to redistribute income toward lower-income retirees, often women, who have higher rates of elderly poverty than men. Regressivity is redistribution from lower- to higher-income groups.

Individual accounts can be designed to redistribute income, for example, through government subsidies to the accounts of workers with low earnings, but this is rarely done. Individual accounts are usually considered to be neutral in their effects on the distribution of income, being neither progressive nor regressive. This is indeed the case when the rate of return received on workers' account balances, net of expenses and taxes, is constant across income classes. That situation would occur if administrative costs were allocated equally across dollars invested in the same portfolio, and if annuitization of benefits recognized differences in life expectancy associated with different income classes. While plans could be designed with those features, frequently none of them are present.

In actual practice, individual accounts may be regressive (Turner 2000). Some regressive aspects of these plans affect the accrual of account balances, and others result from the annuitization of account balances. Other issues arise for voluntary carve-outs because of the relationship between social security and individual accounts. The following discussion considers causes of regressivity and possible remedies.

Effects on Account Balances

Regressivity in individual accounts can be the result of fees that fall disproportionately on low-wage workers. Alternatively, regressivity can result because low-wage workers invest more conservatively and end up with lower account balances relative to their contributions because of the lower returns (before fees) that they receive.

Fees

Individual accounts may penalize low-income workers through the way charges for expenses are allocated. The costs of processing contributions, keeping records, managing investments, and paying benefits are primarily fixed per worker and do not vary by transaction size or account balance. Charges levied by for-profit service providers, when not otherwise constrained by regulation, tend to follow the incidence of costs, with small accounts often having higher charges relative to assets than large accounts. Thus, the regulation of the fee structure may be an important policy issue.

Some individual accounts in Australia and the United Kingdom impose a set entrance fee for opening an account. Individual account providers in Chile charge both fixed and variable costs. In some plans, the fee diminishes as a percentage of the balance for large accounts, or fixed charges are waived for larger balances. Mutual funds in the United States often charge fixed fees for small accounts, with bigger accounts being charged fees that are a lower percentage of assets.

Over the period 1981–1990, the average net rate of return for a worker with the maximum eligible earnings in one of the Chilean pension funds was 10.4 percent, and that for a worker with minimum eligible earnings was 9.2 percent. The difference was due to the fee structure (Habitat 1991). Low-income workers on average actually received only 7.5 percent across funds, compared to 10 percent for high-income workers (Vittas and Iglesias 1991). This is a substantial difference, having a large effect on retirement benefits when compounded over a worker's career.

Government intervention, however, can eliminate this source of regressivity. The fixed costs of accounts can be borne by the government and spread across workers in proportion to their account balances. This can be done, for example, if the government acts as a clearinghouse by collecting contributions and distributing them to pension fund managers, as in Sweden.

There are other sources of regressivity in both mandatory individual account and defined benefit systems. For example, in both programs, when benefits are annuitized using uniform annuity conversion rates, income is redistributed from low-income to high-income workers because the latter outlive their low-income counterparts.

Progressive taxation

Upper-income contributors benefit proportionately more per dollar of account balance than do lower-income contributors when there is a progressive income tax system—one in which higher-income workers pay higher marginal income tax rates—and when contributions to individual accounts and the investment earnings on those accounts receive preferential tax treatment. The amount of tax subsidy per dollar contributed is the same for low- and high-income workers if a tax credit rather than a tax deduction is offered, but that approach costs the government a lot in lost tax revenue and is rarely used.

Risk preference

People differ in their preferences for risk-bearing. It is sometimes argued that a positive aspect of individual accounts with portfolio choice is that individuals can choose the amount of risk that matches their risk preference. A weakness, however, is that participants are generally poorly informed about investments, and, compared with professional money managers, tend to select portfolios that are lower in risk and in return.

Data from the Thrift Savings Plan for U.S. federal government workers suggest that lower-income workers tend to pick more conservative portfolios and receive lower rates of return (Hinz, McCarthy, and Turner 1996). These data may understate the difference between income classes over workers' lifetimes because the upper-income work-

Table 7.1 Rate of Return on an Individual Account Plan with Portfolio Choice, by Income Level

Annual salary ($)	Average rate of return (%)
Less than 20,000	11.3
20,000–29,999	11.9
30,000–39,999	12.0
40,000–49,999	11.8
50,000–59,999	12.3
60,000–69,999	12.3
70,000 or more	12.4

SOURCE: U.S. Thrift Savings Plan data for 1990 (Hinz, McCarthy, and Turner 1996).

ers in the cross-sectional data tend to be older, and their risk aversion may increase as they near retirement. Nonetheless, the difference of 100 basis points (1 percentage point) between the lowest and highest income groups, as shown in Table 7.1, if it persisted over a worker's career, would make a considerable difference in retirement income. Thus, self-management of individual accounts causes the accounts to be regressive because lower-income workers tend to be less sophisticated in managing their accounts and tend to receive lower rates of return.

Annuitization

Annuitization of account balances at retirement insures workers against the risk of outliving their resources. How this is accomplished, however, may add regressive elements to individual accounts. When the accounts annuitize benefits on a uniform basis and do not take into consideration the longer life expectancy associated with higher income, they redistribute toward upper-income workers. When comparing within a gender group, there is a clear pattern of upper-income workers having greater life expectancy. When considering both men and women, however, the connection between income and life expectancy is not as clear. Women have longer life expectancy than men but tend to have lower income.

Insurance companies in Chile, but not in most countries with mandatory individual accounts, consider personal characteristics, including gender, in determining the level of annuity benefits provided by an account balance. This limits regressivity when comparing high- versus low-income workers within a single gender, but at the cost of lower retirement benefits for women than would be the case if unisex life tables were used to calculate annuitized benefits.

The transaction costs associated with an individual worker purchasing an annuity are largely fixed and do not depend on the size of the account balance being annuitized. Thus, these costs have a regressive effect when charged on an individual basis. Annuity charges in Chile are a source of regressivity: larger commissions relative to annuity payments are often charged to lower-income workers (Vittas and Iglesias 1991).

Annuity prices vary across insurance companies. If participants are required to shop for an annuity, as in Chile, low-income workers may be adversely affected. If such individuals are less sophisticated in purchasing annuities than people with higher incomes, they tend to receive a less favorable price. Because lower-income workers have less to save by finding the best price, due to their relatively small account balances, and because the investigation may be particularly difficult for them if they lack financial knowledge, they would tend to be less successful in their searches.

Most mandatory individual accounts allow workers to avoid the regressive effects of annuitization by taking a phased withdrawal of benefits. Providing this option, however, increases the problem of adverse selection in the annuity market and works in a regressive way against low-income participants. Because people who expect to be long-lived are more likely to buy annuities, insurers price the product on the assumption that their purchasers are long-lived. These prices may be actuarially fair for upper-income workers with long life expectancies; the problem is that the high price keeps low-income workers out of the annuity market and deprives them of the protection traditional social insurance plans provide against the risk of outliving one's resources. Not requiring annuitization, however, allows less affluent workers who die relatively young to bequeath some of their retirement income to their survivors, which may be the only form of survivors benefits provided by an individual account system (Box 7.2).

Voluntary Carve-Outs

Although voluntary carve-outs can be structured in different ways, they generally are not as favorable for low-income as for high-income workers. With voluntary annuitization, adverse selection occurs because of the longer life expectancy of high-income participants. Social security forms a larger share of retirement income for individuals with low incomes than for those with high incomes, so lower-income workers are more affected by the change in risk-bearing caused by the carve-out accounts. Disability benefits tend to be more important to low-income labor and may be less generous under voluntary individual carve-out arrangements. If primarily upper-income workers establish individual accounts but government general revenues are used to pay transition costs, the benefits of the system would be going to upper-income workers, while all workers would be paying for the transition.

Box 7.2 The Effect of Increases in Life Expectancy on Social Security Benefits with a Voluntary Carve-Out

Increases in life expectancy are a cause of Social Security's projected insolvency. As people live longer, they receive benefits for more years. When no countervailing changes in the program are made, longer life expectancy eventually leads to financing problems. Sweden deals with this issue by indexing social security benefits to life expectancy, since increases in life expectancy reduce the initial benefit retirees receive.

Private account plans do not face this source of financial insolvency caused by increasing life expectancy. Rather, the monetary burden of greater longevity is typically borne by workers individually. When annuity providers anticipate that people will live longer in retirement, they reduce the annual benefits they provide for a given account balance and retirement age. Workers may then decide to work longer and postpone retirement.

How does an individual account of the type proposed by President Bush deal with increased life expectancy? Under the president's plan, individuals may voluntarily divert part of their contributions from Social Security into a private account. This account would be invested in the financial markets and yield a balance at retirement.

Diverting part of one's Social Security contributions to a private account would result in reduced Social Security benefits at retirement. The Social Security Administration (SSA) would calculate the decrease in benefits based on a hypothetical account established for each person who chooses a private account. This hypothetical account would be credited with the actual contributions made by the person to the private account. It also would be credited with a set interest rate on the hypothetical balance, for example, 3 percent above inflation.

At retirement, the hypothetical account balance resulting from the crediting of contributions and interest would be converted into a hypothetical annuity. This would be based on a unisex life table reflecting life expectancy at retirement as of that time. The annuitized monthly benefit calculated for the hypothetical account would be subtracted from the individual's Social Security monthly benefit

Box 7.2 (continued)

that the person would have received had he or she not chosen to contribute to the private account. The individual would receive the reduced Social Security benefit resulting from this calculation.

Under this plan, life expectancy increases would be reflected in the life table used to annuitize the hypothetical individual account and would reduce the monthly benefit calculated for the hypothetical account. Then, the hypothetical monthly benefit that has been reduced by the increase in life expectancy would be subtracted from the person's Social Security benefit, as previously described. Thus, increases in life expectancy would reduce the annuitized benefit from the hypothetical account, but they would augment by an equal amount the Social Security benefit received by the worker taking the individual account. Thus, if an increase in life expectancy before retirement age reduced the benefits calculated from the hypothetical account by $10 a month, Social Security benefits would increase by $10 a month.

The net result is that the person who chooses the private account does not bear the effect of increases in life expectancy—the reduction in the benefit from the hypothetical account is exactly offset by an increase in his or her Social Security benefit. The net impact for the Social Security trust fund, however, is that it bears the higher benefit cost due to increased life expectancy for those persons taking individual accounts.

The president's plan thus does nothing to solve the problem of increased life expectancy raising Social Security benefit costs. Rather, the cost of greater longevity for individual account participants would be borne by Social Security out of increased benefit payments. Thus, the carve-out private accounts the president has proposed would destabilize Social Security's financing as life expectancy increases, eventually necessitating further changes in program financing or benefits. This effect would not occur with add-on private accounts. That type of private account does not have the complex problem of determining the amount by which Social Security benefits would be offset (the "claw back") for participants taking those accounts.

Progressive Features

Individual accounts could be structured so that they are progressive, with, for example, part of the contributions of higher-income workers being used to subsidize the accounts of lower-income workers. Some individual accounts do have explicitly progressive elements. The government can make periodic flat payments to all accounts, as is done in Mexico. That contribution provides a relatively large subsidy for low-income workers with small accounts. The plan can also be structured to have the government offer matching contributions that phase out at higher income levels. In Australia, the government makes a contribution of up to AUD$1,000 per year to low-income workers who make voluntary payments on top of the mandatory ones for their individual accounts (Pensions Policy Institute 2003). In Sweden, the government provides pension contributions out of general revenue on behalf of persons serving in the military, students, and those receiving disability benefits.

BENEFIT PROTECTION FOR WOMEN

With individual accounts, issues arise as to the benefits a woman receives as a divorcée, as a spouse of a retired worker, and as a widow. What types of benefit protection are available to women, and are those protections mandatory? Australia and the United Kingdom both permit, but do not require, the splitting of pension assets in divorce proceedings. Sweden allows a husband to assign his pension contributions to his wife's account, or a wife to her husband's. Sweden also provides contributions out of general revenue for women who are not working because they are taking care of children.

An issue in calculating annuities concerns to what extent variations in life expectancy arising from factors other than age should be taken into account. Notably, should longevity differences associated with gender be recognized? Not acknowledging this differential can be considered a form of sex discrimination against men (McCarthy and Turner 1993). However, because women have lower average retirement benefits than men, public policy generally determines that annuities should be provided on a unisex basis. To do otherwise would exacerbate the disadvantage in retirement benefits that women already experience.

Benefit protection for women can also be provided through survivors benefits. Sweden and Australia do not require that such benefits be provided, while Chile does in the case of men for their wives if the men receive their benefits in the form of an annuity.

Individual accounts in Latin America sometimes permit women to withdraw benefits at a younger age than men. Chile is an example: women can take benefits at age 60, while men must wait until 65 unless they have accumulated a sufficient amount to qualify for early retirement. If women's retirement age were raised five years to equal that of men, their monthly benefits would increase by about 50 percent even if they did not work any more time, simply because of the five extra years of interest accumulation and the five fewer years of benefit payouts (James, Edwards, and Wong 2003).

With voluntary carve-outs, as proposed in the United States, questions have arisen as to whether the account balances of husbands and wives that have accrued during marriage would be split at divorce. With these accounts, however, there is an associated liability, which is the offset against future Social Security benefits. Splitting the liability could result in a divorced wife receiving a liability that exceeded the benefits she received.

ANNUITIZATION OF BENEFITS

Returning to the theme of risks in individual accounts, financial market risk affects individual account pensions at three points. The first time is during the accumulation phase, because of the risk in equity and bond markets. The second impact is on the initial annuitized benefit at the stage that the account is converted into an annuity, because of fluctuations in interest rates used for the calculations. And the third is during retirement, when the real value of benefits received is affected because of the risks of inflation and of the bankruptcy of insurance companies providing annuities with inadequate reinsurance. With regard to inflation, defined benefit social security plans frequently provide indexed

> **Box 7.3   Interest Rates and the Conversion
> of an Individual Account into an Annuity**
>
> The amount of pension benefits paid out annually from an individual account plan that has been annuitized depends on the interest rate at the time the account balance is annuitized. A pension annuity is a series of monthly payments paid until death. Sudden changes in interest rates just before retirement may significantly affect the level of benefits the individual receives. A drop in interest rates will reduce the pension benefit payable from a given account balance. However, the amount of capital to be converted may also be affected by the change in interest rates: for example, a decrease in interest rates causes an increase in the value of bonds. The net effect of a change in interest rates on the level of benefits cannot be determined in the abstract; it depends on the associated changes in capital market valuations of the assets held in the account.

annuities, as in the United States, but that is rarely done with individual accounts (Chile being an exception).

Burtless (2000b) examined the first two sources of risk in the United States over the years from 1911 to 1999 and found considerable investment risk stemming from variation in the price of annuities, as well as from financial market risk in the value of account balances. Large fluctuations in income replacement rates for retirees can result from variations in the interest rates used to calculate annuities (Box 7.3).

Some degree of mandatory annuitization may be viewed as desirable to ensure that workers will not outlive their retirement savings. However, it is not required in many countries with mandatory individual accounts (Table 7.2). Among the mandatory individual accounts in Latin America, seven countries allow their retirees to either purchase an annuity or to take programmed withdrawals throughout retirement, while two countries require annuity purchases (Kritzer 2000).[2] The compulsory individual accounts in Hungary and Poland require annuitization with private insurers (World Bank 2000). Sweden mandates annuity purchases through the government but gives workers consider-

Table 7.2 A Sampling of Countries with and without Mandatory Annuitization of Individual Accounts, 2000

Countries with mandatory annuitization	Countries without mandatory annuitization
Bolivia	Argentina
Hungary	Australia
Poland	Chile
Sweden	Colombia
UK (at age 75)	El Salvador
Uruguay	Hong Kong

SOURCE: Kritzer (2000) and author's compilation.

able flexibility as to when those are made (Turner 2004). When annuities are purchased through private insurers, the government may need to provide some form of insurance in case the insurer is unable to meet its benefit commitments.

The United Kingdom permits the gradual purchase over time of fixed annuities. Retirees can take a tax-free lump sum of up to a quarter of their accumulated contracted-out individual account. They can draw down the rest of the fund gradually after retirement, but they must buy an annuity with the remainder by age 75. Australia allows participants to take their mandatory individual account benefit either as an annuity or as a lump sum benefit. Tax laws provide substantial incentives to take it as an annuity, but most people take a lump sum (Mitchell and Piggott 2000).

Workers could be permitted to take a lump sum of part of their account if they were able to provide an annuity of sufficient generosity with the remainder, with that level possibly being tied to average wages in the economy. Exceptions to mandatory annuitization might be offered to the terminally ill (Mackenzie 2002).

Mandatory annuity purchases reduce annuity prices by eliminating adverse selection and expanding the market to cover individuals regardless of health and life expectancy. Compulsory annuities insure that individuals will not spend all of their resources in the early years of retirement. However, mandatory annuities cause redistribution from low- to high-income individuals because of the positive correlation of life expectancy with income within gender groups (Brown 1999).

It is often argued that benefit levels in individual accounts are less sensitive to demographic change than are defined benefit systems. Actually, both systems are equally sensitive to increases in longevity, which raise the cost of providing a given level of annuitized benefits. In a defined benefit system, this occurs through increased costs, while in individual accounts its direct effect is a reduction in benefits.

ANNUITIZATION AND LONGEVITY RISK: CONVERSION RATE GUARANTEES FOR ANNUITIES

Variations in interest rates can have a large impact on the level of annual pension benefits received. For a 65-year-old, a 4 percent interest rate generates annual payments of $686 per $10,000 annuitized. This amount rises to $830 at 6 percent and to $982 at 8 percent (Ameriks 2002). Higher interest rates increase annual payments because the income produced by the account balance invested at those rates will be greater. Thus, if a 65-year-old had an account balance of $100,000 and the interest rate at the time of conversion was 4 percent, he or she would receive annual payments of $6,860 and monthly payments of approximately $570, which would continue at that level until death.

Under a guaranteed annuity conversion option, a pension plan promises to convert a worker's account balance to a life annuity at a fixed interest rate, or at an interest rate no lower than a fixed minimum. (See Appendix A at the end of the book for a discussion of rate-of-return guarantees.) A more extensive guarantee would also take into account the mortality table used. If the annuity rates provided under the guarantee are more beneficial to the participant than the prevailing market rates, the plan, employer, or some other entity must make up the difference in the purchase price of the annuity.

The protection of pensioners provided by an interest rate guarantee could be undermined if insurance companies were free to choose mortality tables: the firms could choose a mortality table to offset the effect of low interest rates. Both the interest rates and the mortality tables used in the conversion would need to be regulated. For example, when converting an annuity stream to a lump sum payment, ERISA specifies the discount rate and life table valuation factors in discounting retirement benefits in U.S. private sector pension plans. For distributions in 2001, ERISA established the 30-year Treasury securities interest rate as the maximum discount rate in computing present value. For that year, ERISA also required the use of the 1983 Group Annuity Mortality unisex table in present value computations. Internal Revenue Service (IRS) Revenue Ruling 2001-62, issued on December 31, 2001, requires defined benefit plans to adopt a new mortality table for calculating the minimum present value of lump sum benefits. The new table is the 1994 Group Annuity Reserving Table (94 GAR), which is adjusted on a unisex basis and projected to the year 2002. The present value of the annuity computed using this interest rate and mortality table is the minimum the plan could pay a participant. Annuity conversion guarantees are not an issue with traditional social security plans because those plans specify the benefit level, so the participant does not bear any interest rate risk.

PLANS PROVIDING AN ANNUITY CONVERSION RATE GUARANTEE

Although some private sector voluntary individual accounts and some mandatory plans provide a rate-of-return guarantee for converting an individual account balance to an annuity, most do not. The following countries provide an example of the variety of practice.

Argentina

Argentine insurance companies are required to use a 4 percent nominal rate for annuity pricing for mandatory individual accounts. The Argentine annuity allows the holder to share in returns in excess of 4 percent (World Bank 2000).

Latin America

In all other Latin American countries with individual accounts than Argentina, the interest rate for conversion of the account balance to an annuity varies with the market. Chile provides a government guarantee of annuities in payment, which promises a certain level of benefits against default of the insurance company.

Sweden

Workers have a choice between annuitization through the government, with a guaranteed conversion rate of at least 3 percent, or purchasing a variable annuity, with the annuity recalculated annually (Engström and Westerberg 2003). A variable annuity guarantees payment until death, but the level of benefits fluctuates with the value of the underlying investments. Thus, a variable annuity provides insurance against the risk of outliving one's resources, but it does not provide a guaranteed level of benefits.

Switzerland

Until recently, Switzerland's rate for converting account balances to annuities was 7.2 percent if benefits were taken at age 65. This meant that the annual annuity benefit had to equal at least 7.2 percent of the worker's account balance. Thus, the guarantee, in effect, jointly guaranteed the mortality rates and the interest rates used for calculating annuities. It mandated a sex-neutral conversion. Employers have lobbied the government to reduce this return to reflect low interest rates and diminished mortality rates. In response, the government has decided to decrease the conversion rate at age 65 to 6.4 percent by 2011 to take into account the increase in life expectancy (Hewitt Associates 2002).

United Kingdom

The United Kingdom does not have a rate-of-return guarantee for the annuitization of its contracted-out individual accounts. People must annuitize with private life insurance companies that vary the price of annuities based on the market interest rate. To facilitate greater flexibility with respect to interest rate risk for annuitization, people are allowed a window up to age 75 before they are required to annuitize their accounts.

Conversion rate guarantees for annuitizing account balances were popular in the United Kingdom in the 1970s and 1980s when long-term interest rates were high (Boyle and Hardy 2002). Insurance companies apparently assumed that interest rates would remain high, and thus that the guarantees would never become active. In the early 1990s, when long-term interest rates began to fall, the guarantees became a concern. Two other factors added to the cost of these guarantees. First, strong stock markets meant the amounts to which the guarantees applied increased considerably. Second, the mortality assumption implicit in the guarantee did not reflect the improvement in mortality that was occurring.

United States

While conversion rate guarantees are unusual in the United States, the United Methodist Church of the United States since 1982 has guaranteed an interest rate that is the higher of the following two options: either 8 percent, or the market interest rate for annuitizing the account balances of persons in its Ministerial Pension Plan. Participants are required to annuitize at least 75 percent of their account balances. Because of the cost of that guarantee during a period of low interest rates, it is being phased out; starting in July 2003, it was only offered to persons who had at least 35 years of service or who were aged 62 by July 1, 2003. This guarantee is backed by a reserve fund.

ALTERNATIVE APPROACHES

Fixed-rate guarantees are vulnerable to falls in interest rates. While they may be maintained for long periods when rates are stable, they may be revised or ended during periods of low interest rates. Alternative strategies can be used to limit the interest rate risk for participants associated with annuity conversions for individual account plans. One approach is to allow workers to partially annuitize in several steps, which reduces the risk associated with completely annuitizing at a single point in time. Another tactic is to permit individuals to initially take phased withdrawals and to later take an annuity, giving workers greater flexibility in picking the point at which they annuitize.

TAX POLICY TOWARD INDIVIDUAL ACCOUNTS

Favorable tax treatment is generally used by countries with well-developed pension systems to encourage worker participation (Reagan and Turner 1997). Such an inducement presumably is not needed for mandatory individual accounts since participation in them is required. Thus, it might be expected that mandatory individual accounts would not receive preferential tax treatment. That is not the case. Other issues that may hold reasons for granting favorable tax treatment include the fairness of the taxation of mandatory pensions versus other forms of retirement income, and the need to provide incentives for participation because of contribution evasion by workers and employers.

Pensions can be taxed at three points in the process of accumulating assets and paying benefits: contributions, investment earnings, and withdrawals. The tax treatment of individual accounts can affect worker participation, the forms of payout, and benefit levels (NASI 2005).

Contribution Evasion

One of the reasons for providing favorable tax treatment of mandatory pensions is to address contribution evasion, which is the nonpayment of contributions to compulsory plans. It occurs because of interacting factors affecting workers and employers and because of the failure of government enforcement. Contribution evasion depends in part on whether people view mandatory payments to individual accounts as a tax (Burkhauser and Turner 1985). Consequently, this issue is an important aspect of tax policy toward mandatory individual accounts (Bailey and Turner 2001; see Appendix B).

Contribution evasion is a problem in many social security programs, and favorable tax treatment may reduce the extent to which it occurs. Tax advantages may be provided to encourage participation in mandatory plans and as a matter of tax equity when plans that are voluntary receive preferential tax treatment.

Tax evasion in the mandatory individual account systems in Latin America is a serious problem. Underlying factors appear to be the high level of mandatory contributions and the greater liquidity of other forms of savings (Gill, Packard, and Yermo 2005).

Fundamental Principles of Pension Taxation

Three fundamental principles apply to the taxation of most pensions in the United States and in the majority of other countries providing favorable tax treatment for pensions:

1) Contributions are tax-exempt (excluded from income) or tax-deductible (E, for "exempt").

2) Pension investment earnings are tax-exempt until withdrawn (E).

3) Pension benefits are taxable (T, for "taxable").

This approach to the taxation of pensions is sometimes called the EET model. It is used, for example, by Chile for its mandatory individual accounts. This is the most commonly used method for taxing pensions. With this framework, tax payments are deferred until benefits are received in retirement, presumably for consumption.

Consumption Taxation

The tax treatment of pensions where the tax is levied only at the point of benefit receipt moves countries toward a consumption tax system rather than an income tax system, assuming that benefit payments are consumed rather than saved. Under a consumption tax, retirees generally pay higher taxes than under an income tax raising equal revenue nationally. With this approach, consumption expenditures are taxed but savings, including investment earnings, are not. Earnings set aside through a pension are not taxed until received in retirement, when they are presumably consumed, which is how they would be treated under a consumption tax. A consumption tax avoids double taxation of savings (on the initial income that is saved and on the subsequent investment income) and thus does not distort the decision between current and future consumption. This is a desirable aspect of a tax system, given the concern in many countries that people do not save adequately.

With an income tax approach, employer contributions and pension investment earnings would be taxed but benefit payments would not. The consumption tax approach for pensions is not used in all countries. For example, in the United Kingdom, lump sum benefits are not taxed.

Taxation of Social Security

In the United States, Social Security is taxed differently from private pensions. Social Security receives equal contributions from workers and employers. Workers' contributions are made from after-tax income (they cannot deduct the contributions from their taxable income). Employers' contributions are from before-tax income (they can deduct them from their pretax income, and the contributions are not treated as taxable income to workers). Lower-income retirees are not taxed on their Social Security benefits, while higher-income retirees must include either 50 or 85 percent of their benefits in taxable income, depending on their income level. The effective income tax rate on the employee's share of Social Security contributions, and on the portion of the benefits that the employee must include in taxable income, depends on the employee's income tax rate, which varies across people and is zero in some cases (NASI 2005).

For lower-income retirees, Social Security receives more favorable tax treatment than private pensions, while the opposite holds for higher-income retirees. Tax policy regarding U.S. Social Security benefits complicates the issue of how individual accounts would be taxed as part of the system.

Taxation of Different Benefit Forms

Usually pension benefits are taxed; payments can be received in different forms, however, and tax treatment may be designed to favor one mode over others. Most policy analysts agree that at least a substantial portion of benefits should be paid as an annuity because that insures against the risk of running out of money if the person lives longer than expected. Nonetheless, receiving lump sum payments is popular with workers, and some countries favor that form of receipt by not taxing it.

Taxation of Voluntary Carve-Out Accounts

If contributions from workers to a voluntary carve-out individual account were taken entirely from those workers' payments to Social Security, the contributions would come solely from after-tax income. The usual consumption tax approach of exempting contributions and investment earnings, and taxing benefits (EET), is generally equivalent to taxing contributions and exempting investment earnings and benefits (TEE). They are mathematically equivalent if the tax rate is the same in all periods. Thus, if investment earnings and benefits were not taxed under this proposal, the tax treatment would be equivalent to that of the EET tax treatment of pension plans such as 401(k) plans. However, it would not be equivalent to the tax treatment of Social Security benefits. It would mean that lower-income retirees would be taxed more heavily and higher-income retirees less heavily than under Social Security. Thus, the tax treatment of voluntary carve-out individual accounts could encourage their use by high-income retirees and discourage their use by low-income retirees.

Tax Expenditures

Tax preferences for pensions and Social Security result in lost revenue to the national government, called tax expenditures. The tax expenditure is the cost side of the tax preferences given to pensions. Tax incentives include exempting contributions and investment earnings from income taxation. This approach provides greater inducements for higher-income workers than for lower-income workers in a progressive income tax system because marginal tax rates increase at higher income levels. With a progressive tax system, there may be little incentive for low-income workers to participate (Reagan and Turner 2000).

With add-on individual accounts, tax expenditures would rise to the extent that those accounts increased total tax-favored savings. With voluntary carve-out accounts, tax expenditure would presumably change little, since tax-favored savings through Social Security would be replaced with tax-favored savings in the individual accounts.

CONCLUSIONS

This chapter has surveyed issues concerning the payment of benefits and the tax treatment of individual accounts. There are various options for paying benefits. A major issue is the extent to which workers should be required to annuitize their individual accounts. The provision of inflation protection for retirees is a related issue. An advantage offered by individual accounts is that they can be easily used in conjunction with a program of partial or phased retirement.

Fluctuations in interest rates are a source of risk at the point of retirement when converting an individual account balance to an annuity. The lower the interest rate, the lower are the annual benefits that result from annuitization. This risk can be dealt with in several ways. Sweden has a guaranteed minimum interest rate for converting account balances to annuities, although at a fairly low level. Offering flexibility in the timing of the conversion is another way of dealing with this risk.

Aspects of individual accounts may result in their benefit structure being regressive. Mandatory annuitization results in regressive redistribution because lower-income workers tend to have shorter life expectancies. The structure of fees may cause regressivity because of the fixed costs of managing individual accounts. That problem can be dealt with by mandating that fees be prorated based on account balances.

With mandatory individual accounts, tax issues need to be considered. These may be complex when, as in the United States, Social Security and pension benefits are not taxed the same way, and the tax treatment of Social Security differs for low- and high-income workers. It may be difficult to achieve neutrality between the taxation of Social Security benefits and the taxation of individual account benefits without affecting the relative desirability of employer-provided individual account plans.

Notes

1. The provision of benefits in Sweden is explained in greater detail later in the chapter.
2. The table lists only five Latin American countries as being without mandatory annuitization; it is meant to present examples rather than a complete listing.

8
Summary and Conclusions

Individual accounts as part of social security are being debated in the United States and have been adopted in a number of countries. They can be structured so that they are simple. However, actual individual accounts are generally complex in their design and effects, a fact that is often not appreciated, in part because of their relatively short history in social security systems. Policy analysts, for example, often treat them as not affecting the behavior of workers, being similar to voluntary savings plans. Research on individual account proposals has often focused on stylized versions of these plans, without careful consideration of the effects of their specific features.

With the introduction of individual accounts, many nations around the world have radically changed the way participants accrue, and later receive, retirement income. International comparisons of mandatory individual accounts may be particularly useful for U.S. policymakers because U.S. experience is limited to voluntary plans.

This book analyzes public policy toward mandatory individual accounts. It examines them from numerous perspectives that include international experience and U.S. experience with voluntary accounts, and economic theory. Selective issues from each chapter are summarized in the following discussion.

Policy analysts and reformers in a number of countries have made great strides in developing ways of providing retirement income through individual accounts. Reformers desiring to add individual accounts to a traditional system of social security now have a wide range of options from which to choose, with large differences across countries in approaches that have been taken. Major distinctions depend on whether they are add-ons to or carve-outs from social security and whether they are mandatory or voluntary.

PERSPECTIVES FROM OTHER NATIONS

Individual accounts, used as part of social security, have grown considerably in importance in several regions of the world. Four pathways have been used to encourage the provision of individual accounts (Rein and Turner 2001). They are 1) voluntary with tax incentives, 2) voluntary carve-outs from social security, 3) collective bargaining, and 4) mandatory. This book focuses on voluntary carve-outs from social security and the mandatory approach. For policy analysts desiring to increase retirement savings, voluntary plans can be an alternative to mandatory ones and are generally tried first.

A second way of categorizing individual accounts is the relationship approach whereby individual accounts can be add-ons to or carve-outs from social security. Voluntary carve-out accounts reduce social security benefits and contributions, while mandatory add-on accounts do not affect the social security system but require more contributions.

Combining the pathways and the relationship approaches, individual accounts can be used as part of social security in five ways: 1) voluntary carve-outs that partially replace social security, 2) mandatory add-ons to social security, 3) mandatory carve-outs that partially replace social security, 4) voluntary carve-outs that fully replace social security, and 5) mandatory carve-outs that fully replace social security. Because of the focus on the U.S. debate, this book only considers voluntary carve-outs that partially replace social security and mandatory add-ons.

A third way of categorizing individual accounts is according to how they are managed. Individual accounts can be managed in at least three ways. First, they can be managed by pension fund management companies. In Chile and Mexico, individual workers choose a pension fund management company and direct their employer to send the individual's contribution to that company each month. Second, individual accounts can be managed by employers, as in Australia and Switzerland. Third, the government can play a major role. In Sweden and Poland, the government serves as a clearinghouse, to which employers send their workers' contributions. The government serves as a record keeper and disburses the appropriate amounts to each of the mutual funds in which each worker has elected to invest. In keeping with the U.S. debate, this book focuses on the third approach, in which the government serves as a clearinghouse.

RISK AND PRIVATIZATION

An important criterion in judging social security reforms is the extent to which they meet the income needs of low- and middle-income workers. Social security should provide a stable and secure retirement income for these people. For this reason, the role of risk is important in assessing different retirement income options. It is not possible to conclude that one system is the best for all countries because the risk inherent in the traditional defined benefit social security system varies across nations, as does the risk in the financial markets in which the citizens of a country invest. Even in the high-income nations of the OECD, it is not possible to conclude that one system would be superior because the social security programs already in place in these countries vary considerably. In the international context, an important characteristic of the U.S. Social Security system is the low level of benefits it provides relative to preretirement income. This feature of the U.S. Social Security system is important to keep in mind when considering individual accounts.

Individual accounts are generally less secure for participants than are traditional defined benefit social security plans in high-income countries, such as the United States. Individual accounts are riskier in terms of investment risk, agency risk, individual management risk, the risk of adverse labor market outcomes, disability risk, the risk of premature death, replacement rate risk, annuitization (interest rate) risk, longevity risk, and inflation risk. Defined benefit plans are riskier in terms of dependency rate risk, and for younger workers they are riskier in terms of policy risk. Typically, for workers age 55 and older, there is little policy risk in defined benefit social security plans.

In Appendix A, rate-of-return guarantees for individual account investments are discussed. The argument for rate-of-return guarantees is stronger for carve-out than for add-on accounts because carve-out accounts are replacing part of the traditional social security program. (However, rate-of-return guarantees may be difficult to maintain during prolonged market downturns.) Rate-of-return guarantees are also more important for carve-out accounts than for add-on accounts if the accounts provide a relatively substantial part of retirement income.

Privatization of social security by incorporating individual accounts appeals to some people on both economic and ideological grounds. From the economic standpoint, it is argued that privatizing social security would increase national savings and economic growth. With a declining internal rate of return to pay-as-you-go social security due to slowing population and productivity growth, there is political support for reducing the role of traditional social security programs. Ideologically, privatizing social security is favored by some because it would lessen the role of the government and give people greater responsibility and choice. However, individual accounts that are voluntary carve-outs reduce the secure base provided by traditional social security programs, which in the case of U.S. Social Security is already rather low. It is difficult to construct voluntary carve-out accounts so that they are age- and gender-neutral and are neutral in their effects on the financing of the traditional social security program. Further, individual accounts are subject to some of the same criticisms of traditional social security systems. The level of annuitized benefits they provide is subject to longevity risk, and annuitized benefits tend to redistribute income to higher income people.

The extent to which individual accounts have supplanted social security programs has varied, with a few countries fully replacing their social security systems but a larger number partially changing them. Until the reform in Chile in 1981, however, no country had private administration of a social security individual accounts program. After observing the Chilean social security reform for more than a decade, other Latin American countries introduced individual accounts as part of their social security systems.

Following the 1991 breakup of the Soviet Union, the benefits provided by existing and recently created social protection systems of the new countries were not sufficient to handle the economic problems facing the region's retirees. Many of these countries are rethinking their social security programs, with some adopting mandatory individual accounts. Comprehensive social security reforms have been implemented in Croatia, the Czech Republic, Hungary, Latvia, and Poland. Russia has introduced mandatory individual accounts, based in part on the system in Sweden.

PROBLEMS RELATED TO FINANCIAL MANAGEMENT

While the term "tiers" is often used to describe different parts of a retirement income system, it is used in this book to refer to three levels of management of participants' investments in individual accounts. These are financial management by corporations, by mutual funds, and by individual participants. Problems for individual account participants occur at all three levels.

In considering financial management by corporations, the question arises of whether participants in individual accounts, and other investors, have sufficient safeguards. The collapse of Enron Corporation exposed weaknesses in financial protections for U.S. investors. For mutual funds, the level of fees participants pay and the transparency of those fees need to be evaluated. Although individual accounts are sometimes considered to be transparent, the fees participants pay are generally far from transparent.

In addition, individual accounts place a burden of financial market expertise on all workers. Many people are uninformed about investments and financial theory, do not have any interest in pursuing these topics, and are perplexed when required to do so. Such issues can be complex, and even experts do not all agree on some basic strategies, such as how investment portfolios should change as workers age. Many low-income and poorly educated workers have no background in finance and do not even have checking accounts. Financial education may need to be an aspect of an individual account system.

Experience with individual accounts as part of social security in Sweden indicates that frequently workers do not make an investment choice. Many people end up with the default fund for their pension investments (Sweden, Argentina). While some people may not make a choice, others may choose the default fund, thinking that it is the recommended alternative. Consequently, the portfolio held by the default fund is a critical aspect of system design. The default fund in Sweden is heavily invested in equities, and there is no provision to reduce exposure to equity market risk as people approach retirement age. By comparison, in Chile the default funds vary by the age of the worker, with older workers being placed in default funds with less risk.

Compared to professional money managers, individual workers tend to be more conservative and less sophisticated. Various factors may explain why women tend to be more cautious investors of pension funds than men, including the generally lower earnings of women. Investment mistakes made by unsophisticated (and sophisticated) pension participants include insufficient diversification, excessive trading, market timing (trying to anticipate the swings of the market), trading following market changes, and holding what would appear to be too much or too little risk when compared to the investment portfolios of professional investors. Inertia may keep workers from making needed adjustments to their portfolios.

Administrative costs vary significantly among countries with individual accounts. Fees can reduce workers' investments substantially. In most individual account systems, fees paid are not clearly disclosed, and participants have little understanding of how much they have paid in fees.

BEHAVIORAL EFFECTS

Voluntary individual accounts can be designed so as not to have labor market effects. Mandated individual accounts, however, generally may influence aspects of labor supply, and they usually contain regressive features, due in part to the shorter life expectancies of low-wage workers.

Individual accounts may affect hours worked and retirement age. They may have behavioral impacts because of the structure of their administrative expenses, the effects of worker myopia, capital market risks on account balances, and interest rate risks on monthly benefits when benefits are annuitized, with participants possibly timing retirement based on their expectations as to interest rates. If people delay retirement because of declines in the values of their individual accounts, there will be greater difficulties for other workers who are trying to find jobs during an economic downturn.

Furthermore, individual accounts may change worker behavior through their relationship to minimum benefit and poverty programs, which may provide incentives to low-wage employees to evade participation in individual accounts or to spend down those accounts so as to qualify for social assistance benefits. Thus, the impact of individual accounts may depend on the structure of the system as a whole rather than on just the accounts themselves. Further empirical and theoretical research is needed to assess the magnitudes of the effects discussed.

Issues related to contribution evasion and avoidance have implications for the labor market, particularly for lower-wage workers in the informal sector. Contribution evasion and avoidance, reflecting attitudes toward taxation in general, is a problem for employees as well as for the social security system.

BENEFIT PAYOUT

When a worker reaches retirement, the question arises as to how that worker's individual account should be converted into a retirement benefit. Difficult issues need to be addressed concerning the payout options that are provided and whether, for example, all participants should be made to fully annuitize their individual account balances. Alternatively, only annuitization of a minimum amount sufficient to guarantee income above poverty could be required, or phased payments could be an option. The mandatory individual accounts in Sweden give participants flexibility as to when they can start receiving benefits and also allow for partial receipt of benefits, facilitating partial or phased retirement.

Annuitization of benefits provides insurance against outliving one's benefits, but it also tends to be relatively unfavorable to lower-income workers. Lower-income participants (within gender groups) tend to have shorter life expectancy, but women tend to have lower income and higher life expectancy. While traditional social security defined benefit plans typically provide price-indexed benefits, this is uncommon for individual accounts. Social Security in the United States is a bigger percentage of retirement income for low-income workers, and thus any changes in Social Security, including introducing individual accounts, have a bigger effect on them.

Generally, participants in individual accounts wishing to annuitize their balance are affected by interest rate risk because the calculation of their benefit depends on the interest rates prevailing at the time of conversion. A higher interest rate means a higher annuitized benefit. Annuity conversion rate risk in individual accounts can be reduced through rate-of-return guarantees at the point of annuitization. While such guarantees have been fairly common during the accumulation phase, they are not nearly as common for annuity conversions.

Taxation issues need to be considered for individual accounts. Difficult issues arise in attempting to make the tax treatment of individual accounts neutral with respect to both social security benefits and private pension benefits.

TWELVE MYTHS ABOUT INDIVIDUAL ACCOUNTS

A number of myths have been part of the Social Security reform debate. These myths persist because they contain an element of truth. This section discusses myths about voluntary carve-out individual accounts. Some of these myths are true for mandatory or voluntary add-on individual accounts but not for voluntary carve-out accounts. Some of them are true for 401(k) plans or for the Thrift Savings Plan for federal government workers. Some of these myths arise from abstract analysis of idealized situations rather than from an examination of the actual experience of countries that have enacted the types of policies the United States is considering. Some of the myths contain an element of truth that is outweighed by considerations in a more complete analysis.

Myth 1: Voluntary carve-out accounts are like 401(k) plans or like the Thrift Savings Plan for federal government workers.

The element of truth in this myth is that there is a similarity among these types of plans in that all three are examples of individual account plans. However, the popular 401(k) plan and the Thrift Savings Plan are both add-on accounts. Workers participating in those plans participate fully in Social Security—those plans do not reduce the Social Security benefits of workers participating in them.

Myth 2: Voluntary carve-out accounts foster an ownership society.

This myth also contains an element of truth. You own outright an add-on individual account, such as a 401(k) plan or the Thrift Savings Plan. However, a voluntary carve-out plan is a loan. While workers own the amount in the account, the money used to establish the account is a loan. The money contributed to the account is a loan because at retirement workers are required to pay back that amount, with interest, through a reduction in their Social Security benefits.

Myth 3: Voluntary carve-out accounts will increase national savings.

The element of truth in this myth is that add-on accounts may increase national savings. However, voluntary carve-out accounts are much less likely to increase national savings. The worker finances them by debt, which is the implicit borrowing from the Social Security program. On a national basis, the government likely will need to borrow to finance the payment of the benefits of current retirees that would have been financed by the payroll tax payments that no longer are going into Social Security but instead are going into individual accounts.

Myth 4: An individual account will be free from political interference or political risk that arises from changes in government policies.

The element of truth in this myth is that it is possible to construct individual accounts so that they are free from political interference. However, experience in other countries has shown that to not always be the case. For example, in Sweden, the default fund, which is the fund that most new participants invest in, does not invest in Coca-Cola because of the Swedish government's objections to some of its policies. As for political risk, in the United Kingdom the terms of the tradeoff between the reduction in social security benefits and the contribution to the individual account are reset by the government every five years to adjust to changing economic and demographic conditions. This adjustment is subject to error and has added an element of risk to the U.K. system.

Myth 5: People who choose a voluntary carve-out account will be better off because that option expands the range of choice. Since the choice is voluntary, people will only take a voluntary carve-out account if that makes them better off.

Abstract analysis of an idealized situation indicates that people who voluntarily choose an option are by definition made better off by having the option to choose and by their having viewed it to be in their interest to voluntarily choose it. In the United Kingdom, however, many people who have chosen voluntary carve-out accounts have been made worse off by their choice because they were influenced to make a particular choice in what is known as the "mis-selling" scandal. But in the United Kingdom, the negative effects of this problem are limited by the ability of people to return fully to the social security system if they feel that their choice has made them worse off. Proposals in the United States have generally not provided the option of later returning to full participation in Social Security.

Myth 6: Voluntary carve-out accounts will reduce government involvement in the retirement income system.

The element of truth in this myth is that the government would provide a reduced percentage of retirement income. However, the government bureaucracy overseeing the retirement income system would expand substantially. The staffing of the Social Security Administration could easily double because of the record-keeping requirements for voluntary carve-out individual accounts (Hart et al. 2001).

Myth 7: Poor and low-income people would find individual accounts to be a desirable option.

The element of truth in this myth is that poor and low-income people tend not to have investments in the stock market, and having an individual account would diversify their sources of retirement income. However, people that rely entirely on Social Security for their retirement income are not well situated to bear the risk that is inherent in investments in the stock market. The rate of return they receive from Social Security tends to be higher than for higher-income workers because of the progressivity of the Social Security benefit formula. Also, the level of financial literacy in these groups tends to be low, so they would be more prone to errors in managing their accounts.

Myth 8: Individuals will be good financial managers of their individual accounts.

The element of truth is that some individuals will be good financial managers. However, experience with 401(k) plans and with the mandatory individual accounts in Sweden indicates that many individuals make errors in choosing their investments and in the timing of changes in their investments.

Myth 9: Survivors will be better off if workers choose an individual account.

The element of truth is that survivors will be able to inherit the balance of the individual account when workers die, assuming that the individual account has not been annuitized. However, the cost in doing so is that the worker gives up the survivors insurance provided by Social Security. If a person dies young, the balance of his or her individual account would be small, and the survivors clearly would be better off in many situations with the survivors benefits that Social Security provides.

Myth 10: The rate of return a worker receives from the individual account would be higher than what would be received from Social Security.

The element of truth is that stocks earn a higher rate of return than what workers can receive through participation in Social Security. However, if that rate of return is adjusted for the higher risk in stocks, and is adjusted for the higher taxes that ultimately would be needed to pay the transition costs to an individual account system, the rate of return would be essentially the same.

Myth 11: Individual accounts do not redistribute income.

Individual accounts can be constructed as lump sum benefits so that they do not redistribute income. However, when they are annuitized, as they nearly always are, they redistribute income from low- to high-wage workers because high-wage workers tend to have longer life expectancy than do low-wage workers. Because high-wage workers receive the annuitized benefits for more years, the accounts are more valuable to them.

Myth 12: Individual accounts do not affect labor supply and retirement age.

The element of truth in this myth is that individual accounts are not financed by an explicit tax, and thus do not affect labor supply or retirement age through the distorting effect of an explicit tax. However, a high mandatory contribution can function as an implicit tax. Further, for any individual account plan, a sharp downturn in equity markets can cause workers on the verge of retirement to delay retirement. Their change in plans comes at a time when a weak economy has reduced the demand for labor. Thus, older workers are induced to work longer just when firms tend to be laying off workers. Their hanging onto their jobs only increases the number of layoffs that occur in such times.

CONCLUSIONS

An important criterion in judging social security reforms is the extent to which the reforms meet the needs of low- and middle-income workers. Social security should provide these workers a stable, low-risk retirement income. For this reason, the role of risk is important in assessing different retirement income options. And, for the same reason, the risk of add-on individual accounts is less significant in Sweden, with its generous base system, than it would be for voluntary carve-out accounts that would reduce an already modest level of Social Security benefits in the United States.

Individual accounts should not be viewed generically. Policy discussion should delineate whether those accounts are add-ons or carve-outs and whether they are voluntary or mandatory. While voluntary carve-out accounts have appeal in that they preserve an element of choice, in actual functioning—notably in the United Kingdom—serious problems have been encountered in structuring the selection and in participants choosing wisely.

Social security systems must adjust to changing economic and demographic realities. It is safe to conclude that no social security system is without problems—a point, however, that is sometimes overlooked when new systems are being proposed.

The U.S. Social Security program needs to be reformed to restore the balance of contributions and benefits. That problem rightfully ranks high on the national agenda, and it requires changes in traditional benefits and contributions. Individual accounts do not help restore Social Security to solvency, and voluntary carve-out accounts worsen the financing problem over a transition period lasting decades. The arguments advanced for adding individual accounts to Social Security relate to issues of national savings, economic efficiency, and private ownership—areas where there is not a national consensus as to the analysis of the issues, nor as to their significance.

When considering new programs, it is important that their strengths and weaknesses be evaluated, rather than focusing solely on the weaknesses of existing programs. Sufficient time has now passed that the functioning of individual accounts can be evaluated based on lessons learned from the experiences of the United Kingdom and Chile. The Swedish reform is relatively new, so its innovative features have not stood the test of time, though its approach appears to have desirable features with respect to limiting administrative costs and providing flexibility in the receipt of benefits. In both the voluntary carve-out accounts in the United Kingdom and the mandatory carve-out accounts in Chile, the individual account reforms have decreased in popularity: workers have "voted with their feet," and participation in those accounts has declined. In the United Kingdom in 2005, a national pension commission recommended abolishing voluntary carve-out individual accounts.

Mandatory add-on accounts provided on top of a secure base Social Security benefit would not have the problems of carve-out accounts of worsening Social Security financing during the transition and reducing Social Security benefits, nor the problem of how to structure the tradeoff between Social Security benefits and contributions to an individual account. They have some of the desirable features of individual accounts in that they could increase the amount of funded pension savings and raise retirement income, but they would also raise the Social Security payments made by workers, including low-wage workers who may have more pressing financial needs. It can be hoped that the continuing national debate on these issues will benefit from clear thinking as to the strengths and weaknesses of alternative approaches.

Appendix A

Dealing with Financial Market Risk:
Guarantees in Individual Accounts

Guarantees can serve as a way of reducing financial market risks for pension participants. This appendix focuses on rate-of-return guarantees during the accumulation phase. First, the Chilean pension system is examined, to provide examples of different types of guarantees, including those for minimum benefits.

GUARANTEES IN THE CHILEAN SYSTEM

The Chilean government provides four guarantees in its private individual account system. First, it promises a minimum pension to workers who have contributed at least 20 years. This commitment is targeted to long-term, low-wage workers and serves as an antipoverty benefit. Second, it guarantees a lower minimum pension to workers who have contributed less than 20 years. Third, it guarantees a minimum rate of return in case a pension fund management company (an AFP) underperforms the limits set relative to the average rate of return received by other pension funds. Fourth, it ensures payments to pensioners receiving annuitized benefits from any insurance company that becomes bankrupt.

The Chilean AFPs are required to provide a relative rate-of-return guarantee for workers while they are accumulating an account for retirement. This guarantee has served as a model in other countries. In the Chilean AFPs, if the rate of return received by a fund is above or below a band around the average rate of return received by all funds, the worker is credited with the maximum or minimum band rate rather than the actual rate of return. The minimum guarantee on the annualized monthly rate of return is 50 percent of the average real rate of return for all pension funds or below the average by 2 percentage points, whichever is lower. Chilean pension fund managers are required to set aside the excess amount into a profitability reserve fund maintained for each pension fund whenever their real rate of return is 50 percent higher than the mean for all pension funds for the preceding 36 months or exceeds the industry average by 2 percentage points, whichever is higher.

Chile switched to a 36-month averaging period from the 12-month period it initially used in order to encourage investment in portfolios with greater risk and to give fund managers wider range for picking portfolios. A criticism of the guarantee with a 12-month averaging period was that it forced all of the pension funds to have similar portfolios, reducing the choices available to participants. That effect on pension portfolios is called "herding" (Chlon, Góra, and Rutkowski 1999).

The Chilean guarantee is an example of ways that a guarantee can be financed—it has three sources of financial underpinning. Should the rate of return on a pension fund fall below the guaranteed rate of return, the fund manager is required to make up the difference through its profitability reserve fund, which contains revenues from times when the rate of return exceeded the maximum allowed. If the reserve fund is inadequate, the pension fund manager must make up the remaining difference from its own reserve fund, provided by the fund's owners. The fund's owners must maintain a separate reserve fund using their own money, equal to 1 percent of the pension fund's assets, invested in the same portfolio as the pension fund. If that also is inadequate, the government makes up the remaining difference, the pension fund management company is liquidated, and the pension fund accounts are disbursed to other companies. The government, using general tax revenue, serves as guarantor of last resort. The government does not charge a premium but provides that insurance without cost to the pension system. Employers play no role in providing guarantees.

This type of rate-of-return guarantee limits the plan-specific risk to workers, which is the risk that the plan's rate of return differs from the average for all plans. The guarantee has little impact, however, on the bearing of financial market risk, which affects the rates of return received by all plans. For example, during 1995, the average real rate of return in Chile was negative (−2.5 percent) for all pension plans, against which this form of risk-sharing provided no protection.

RATE-OF-RETURN GUARANTEES

The Chilean rate-of-return guarantee is a prominent example of rate-of-return guarantees, but countries with mandatory individual accounts have structured those guarantees in a number of different ways. During the period of work and contributions before retirement, pension guarantees can provide either a minimum level of benefits at retirement or a minimum rate of return. Minimum benefit guarantees can be structured as antipoverty benefits that only affect low-income workers, with a flat guarantee for all workers. Higher-income workers would not be affected because their benefits would exceed the guaranty amount. Alternatively, minimum benefit guarantees can be structured so that the guaranteed amount differs for each worker, depending on how much has been contributed to his or her pension account.

In structuring guarantees, there is a trade-off between the insurance provided by the guarantee and its cost. While the expected cost of a guarantee is an important factor to consider, it can be difficult to determine.

Rate-of-return guarantees may be absolute with a fixed minimum rate of return, or they may be relative to an index. One type of fixed guarantee is the return of principal: a guarantee of a zero nominal rate of return, which is required in Germany and Japan for voluntary individual accounts (Lachance and Mitchell 2003). A more generous promise is to return the real (inflation-adjusted) value of the principal.

The structure of rate-of-return guarantees for individual accounts can be used as a framework for a survey of the guarantees that countries have provided. The design of these plans can be divided into three elements: the measurement of the rate of return guaranteed, the guarantee's payoff characteristics, and the guarantee's financing.

Measurement of the Guaranteed Rate of Return

If one were a planner for a mandatory defined contribution system, the first element of constructing a rate-of-return guarantee would be deciding exactly what is to be guaranteed. The rate-of-return guaranteed can be measured in different ways.

Real or nominal

Uruguay uses a real rate-of-return guarantee for its individual account plans, adjusting for inflation as measured by the change in consumer prices, while Switzerland uses a nominal one.

Fixed or indexed

The guarantee can be a fixed rate of return (either nominal or real) or it can be a rate of return that varies according to a capital market index. The index could be based on the rate of return received on a given asset or portfolio of assets, the actuarial rate of return assumed for an associated defined benefit plan, or the rate of return received by a given group of investors, such as all pension fund managers. The defined contribution plan for teachers in Indiana offers a guarantee based on the actuarial rate of return assumed on the associated defined benefit plan (Turner and Rajnes 2004). Uruguay uses a fixed rate-of-return guarantee, while Chile uses one that varies according to an index.[1]

The averaging period for the guaranteed rate of return

The time dimension on the rate of return can be a fixed period, such as a month, a calendar year, or each consecutive 12-month period, or it can be a cumulative rate of return based on compounding annual rates of return over a longer period. Some plans for government workers in New Zealand use a cumulative rate of return. Before 1999, Chile used an annual rate of return over each consecutive 12-month period. Since then, it has guaranteed a rate of return averaged over rolling 36-month periods. When a longer time period is used, the cost of providing the guarantee declines. This occurs because the volatility of average rates of return is reduced the longer the averaging period. Thus, returns averaged over longer periods are less likely to fall below the guaranteed level.

Explicit or implicit rates of return

A rate-of-return guarantee is equivalent to promising a minimum level of assets in the worker's pension account, given the contributions. Thus, a guarantee of a minimum level of the pension fund implicitly guarantees a minimum rate of return. Chile uses a guarantee based on explicit rates of return, while the guarantee on mandatory individual accounts in Mexico has an implicit rate of return, that being the rate of return that would be sufficient to provide the guaranteed minimum benefit.

The rate of return guaranteed

The rate of return guaranteed may be the actual one received on the pension portfolio of the participant, or it may be a benchmark rate of return. For example, the guarantee could stipulate that you would receive at least a zero rate of return assuming you had invested in the S&P 500, and, regardless of your actual investment, if the S&P 500 index rate of return was lower, you would receive the difference sufficient to raise a portfolio of your amount to a zero rate of return had it been invested in the S&P 500. A benchmark rate of return would eliminate the problem of moral hazard in the selection of investment portfolios by workers, employers, or pension fund managers, and would allow a wider range of portfolios to be selected. With moral hazard, if workers managed their pension portfolios but the pension fund manager provided the guarantee, workers would have an incentive to invest in very risky assets if the guarantee were based on the actual portfolio returns, rather than on a benchmark. By investing in risky assets, they would benefit from the upside potential associated with the high risk but would not have to bear the downside risk since that would be limited by the guarantee.

Generally, forms of investment protection generate moral hazard (Whitehouse 2000). Once the losses from a risk are insured, people will take less care to avoid that risk. Chile uses the actual rate of return received but offers workers little choice as to the portfolio that is guaranteed. Feldstein, Ranguelova, and Samwick (1999) propose a guarantee based on a benchmark, which separates worker choice from moral hazard, allowing participants greater choice as to the investment portfolio.

The Guarantee's Payoff Characteristics

The guarantee's payoff characteristics can be analyzed in terms of the risk and expected return the worker faces when the guarantee is in place.

Risk-sharing in the guarantee

A minimum guarantee (with the possibility of the worker receiving a higher rate of return) may be offered, versus a point guarantee, where the rate of return the worker receives is specified. Guarantees differ with respect to who receives the investment returns when the rate of return is above the promised level. When this occurs, the institution providing the point guarantee, rather than the worker, receives the entire rate of return above the guarantee.

With a minimum guarantee, the worker can receive the entire rate of return above the promised level, or the institution providing the guarantee may receive part of it. In Chile, workers receive the total rate of return above the minimum and below the maximum, but none of the rate of return above the maximum, that amount being deposited into a reserve that is used to fund the rate-of-return guarantee. This is a form of hedging, with the risk of loss being lowered by reducing the potential gain. In Poland, workers receive the entire amount above the minimum guaranteed level. In Switzerland, most mandatory plans pay the fixed guaranteed rate regardless of whether the actual portfolio return is above or below that rate.

The application frequency of the guarantee

The guarantee period determines the point at which the guarantee is exercised. It can be at a fixed interval, such as a quarter or a year, so that it is a series of successive guarantees; alternatively, it can be a cumulative guarantee, so that the period is from the start until the end of the worker's participation, and the guarantee is based on the termination value of the person's account. A cumulative guarantee can provide that the rate must exceed a minimum cumulated rate at the end of every year or only that it must exceed that rate at the end of participation in the plan. Some of the guarantee funds in Hong Kong require a minimum stay in the plan in order to qualify for the guarantee.

The extent of liability of the guarantor

The guarantor, or the party making the guarantee, can have limited or unlimited liability. When the guarantor has limited liability, there is a cap on the expenditure the guarantor is required to make. This is analogous to caps in health insurance policies.

The risk that the guarantee will be changed

The guarantee may be viewed as an enduring promise or as one that is likely to be revised in the future. All commitments have some likelihood that they will be changed, but this probability is greater with fixed rate-of-return guarantees than with relative ones, which have more flexibility. With the bear market in the early 2000s, a number of mandatory individual accounts with fixed nominal guarantees lowered the guarantee rate. For example, Switzerland, which had set its guarantee at 4 percent for many years, reduced that rate to 2.5 percent in 2003.

The type of insurance provided

A guarantee can be set fairly high relative to the expected return (a non-catastrophic guarantee), or it can be set low so that it only provides protection against a low rate of return (a catastrophic guarantee).

Mandatory or voluntary

The guarantee can be mandatory or voluntary, and this aspect can differ for employers and employees. For example, it could be voluntary for employers to offer, but employers could stipulate it for all their employees. Alternatively, it could be mandatory that employers providing a defined contribution plan offer a guarantee as an option, but it could be voluntary for employees to choose that option. In Norway, the parliament proposed, but subsequently rejected, a guarantee that would be voluntary for employers in that they would not be required to provide such a plan, but would be mandatory for workers at firms that chose it. In Hong Kong, the mutual funds may offer a guaranteed fund as an alternative, and it is voluntary for employees to select that option.

The Financial Backing for the Guarantee

Guarantees require a source of funds to provide their financial backing.

Funded or pay-as-you-go

Guarantees can be fully or partially advance-funded or they can be pay-as-you-go financed. The guarantee on mandatory individual accounts in Chile is partially funded, with the government having a residual liability on a pay-as-you-go basis if the private sector funding for guarantees is insufficient.

The party financing the guarantee

A guarantee can be financed by the employee, the employer, the pension fund management firm, or the government. In Chile, the guarantee is partially financed by the employee in that, in some periods, part of the rate of return received on the worker's account is set aside to finance the guarantee. It is partially financed by the pension fund management company, which must set aside some of its own money to finance the guarantee. It also is partially financed by the government, which is the insurer of last resort.

The party insuring the guarantee

The party insuring the guarantee, which is not necessarily the same as the party financing the guarantee, can be an employer, a pension fund provider, an insurance company, or the government. For the United States, Jefferson (2000) has proposed a rate-of-return guarantee for individual accounts financed by employer premiums paid to the Pension Benefit Guaranty Corporation, which would then insure the guarantee.

The Cost of Guarantees

Whether providing a guarantee is a desirable option depends in part on the cost of the guarantee, which varies greatly with its features. Clearly, the higher the rate of return guaranteed, the greater its expected cost. The guarantee of the return of principal has very low cost when applied over a period of years.

The cost of a guarantee of return of principal when the underlying investments are restricted to bonds declines with increases in the investment period and is practically nothing after seven years. The cost of the same guarantee for an asset invested only in equities also falls with the length of the investment period but is still 2.7 percent after 20 years (Maurer and Schlag 2003).

Features of a guarantee that increase the likelihood that it will be effective also raise its expected cost in the following ways.

- A guarantee that restricts the underlying portfolio to bonds is less costly than one that is based on equity investments. Generally, the greater the investment risk, the greater the cost of the guarantee (Lachance and Mitchell 2003).

- A real rate-of-return guarantee of zero (return of real principal) is more expensive than a nominal rate-of-return guarantee of zero because the real return would have to compensate for inflation.

- Similarly, real rate-of-return guarantees of greater than zero tend to be more expensive than nominal rate-of-return guarantees because the former promise automatically to adjust upward (in nominal terms) for changes in inflation.

- Rate-of-return guarantees that apply for short periods (such as a year) are more costly than guarantees for longer periods (such as three years) because fluctuations in rates of return can be averaged out within the longer guarantee period.

- Guarantees in which there is no ceiling on the rate of return received are more expensive to provide than guarantees with a maximum limit, with the excess returns above that point going into a fund to finance the guarantee in the future.

To give an idea of the expense of guarantees, for someone with a 40-year investment horizon who holds a portfolio that is half bonds and half stocks, the cost of guaranteeing the 10-year Treasury bond return would be 0.65 percent of assets annually, nearly doubling to 1.27 percent for an all-stocks portfolio (Lachance and Mitchell 2003). This is expensive, considering that a low-cost equity index mutual fund would have fees of about 0.20 percent of assets annually. If, instead, the guarantee was the return of nominal or real principal, the cost would drop to 0.02 percent for the real principal guarantee and approximately zero for the nominal principal guarantee (Lachance and Mitchell 2003).

What Guarantees Accomplish

The relative and fixed rate-of-return guarantees are designed for different purposes. A relative guarantee ensures that, at a particular point in time, all participants will receive a similar rate of return. It, however, provides no protection against a decline in market rates. A fixed guarantee is designed to protect against declines in market return. However, the three-year decline in world capital markets, starting in 2000, showed the limits to fixed rate-of-return promises. A number of countries with such policies reduced the guaranteed rate. For example, Switzerland, which requires a guaranteed rate of return for its mandatory employer-provided pensions, lowered the rate because of the decline in returns in financial markets.

GUARANTEES IN MANDATORY INDIVIDUAL ACCOUNTS AROUND THE WORLD

Because of concern for the level of financial risk borne by workers, many mandatory defined contribution systems provide guarantees. This survey of rate-of-return guarantees around the world indicates the range of approaches that have been developed. Table A.1 gives an overview, summarizing the presence and types of guarantees found in mandatory defined contribution systems. A few countries with mandatory individual accounts do not offer guarantees (e.g., Australia, Bolivia, Sweden). Among the majority that do provide them, the guarantees can be categorized as either being relative or absolute. Table A.1 is organized by type of guarantee, while the text, which provides greater detail, is organized by region of the world. Countries were selected for discussion so as to provide examples of the different types of guarantees.

Latin America

Uruguay

Uruguay permits both private and government management of pension funds. For the state-owned fund management company, the government guarantees a minimum annual real rate of return equal to 2 percent. If the fund earns less for a year, the government transfers money to the fund to make up the difference. The private pension fund management companies must maintain a guarantee fund, used to supplement pension accounts of workers if the return of their portfolios falls below a defined minimum rate of return: the lower of 2 percent real and the average industry return minus 200 basis points (2 percentage points). This regulation may create a competitive disadvantage for the private companies, which must bear the costs of maintaining the guarantee fund (Mosconi 1997), and seems to have contributed to the dominance of the state-owned fund in the pension industry, which ranks among the most highly concentrated in Latin America.

Table A.1 Guarantees in Mandatory Defined Contribution Systems

Country and type of guarantee	Level of guarantee
Countries with no guarantee	
Australia	
Bolivia	
Latvia	
Mexico	
Sweden	
Countries with an absolute level guarantee	
Denmark (ATP plan)	4.5% nominal
Singapore	2.5% nominal
Switzerland	2.5% nominal
Countries with a relative guarantee	
Argentina (private only)	70% of the average nominal rate of return for all plans or 2 percentage points below, whichever is lower
Chile	50% of the average real rate of return for all plans or 2 percentage points below, whichever is lower
Colombia	Minimum based on a composite of the average performance of all pension funds and the performance of the country's three stock exchanges
Hungary	Minimum rate set each year, depending in part on expected market rates
Poland	50% of the average nominal rate of return for all plans or 4 percentage points below the average, whichever is lower
Uruguay (private only)	2 percent real or the average return of the system minus 2 percentage points (200 basis points), whichever is lower

NOTE: This table necessarily involves some simplification in its categorization and description of guarantees. Refer to the text for a fuller description of the individual countries.
SOURCE: Turner and Rajnes (2001).

In setting an absolute rate-of-return guarantee, Uruguay differs from most other reform countries in the region (Argentina's absolute guarantee applies only to the state-run pension fund manager, Administradoras de Fondos de Jubilaciones y Pensiones [AFJP]). The return is calculated monthly on a rolling basis.

Mexico

Mexico does not provide an explicit rate-of-return guarantee, but, during the transition phase of its system, it provides an implicit assurance through its minimum pension guarantee. While "transition" may suggest a short time period, this phase actually lasts decades. Workers who were already participating in the old system when the reform was instituted have the option when they attain age 65 (with 25 years of contributions) of receiving a benefit based on their defined contribution plan or on their former social security plan. If the former social security's plan benefits are higher, the defined contribution funds are taxed at 100 percent and the government pays the old benefit level. The government decided to offer this "life-switch" option instead of acknowledging the previous contributions of transition workers through recognition bonds, as in Chile. There, workers were given special government bonds to compensate them for the benefits they had accrued under the old social security system. Once the old system is completely phased out, this guarantee will no longer be provided. The government supervisory organization, Comisión Nacional del Sistema de Ahorro para el Retiro (CONSAR), requires that at least 51 percent of a worker's account balance be invested in inflation-linked bonds; this stipulation provides another guarantee aspect of the system (Sinha 1999).

Central and Eastern Europe: Hungary

Hungary has second-tier defined contribution funds, with a traditional defined benefit social security plan constituting the mandatory first tier. Workers are required to choose a fund to which they contribute. Several guarantees apply to these pension funds. First, each year, prospectively, the Private Fund Supervisory Board sets the minimum and maximum rates of return that may be received on fund accounts. Second, at retirement, each worker is guaranteed to receive a minimum benefit from his or her pension fund. Hungary has a mandatory defined benefit pension that will provide a replacement rate of 48.8 percent after 40 years of contributions. The defined contribution plan is guaranteed to provide a pension benefit equal to at least 25 percent of that of the mandatory defined benefit plan after 15 years of contributions (Hungary 1997).

The Hungarian mutual associations that manage pension funds are required to maintain rate-of-return guarantee reserves. If the rate of return on the fund's investments exceeds the maximum rate of return, a portion of the surplus (the portion determined by government decree) is transferred to the return guarantee reserves. If the return on the fund's investments is less than the required minimum return, funds from the reserves are transferred to the worker's individual account. The reserves are required to be no lower than 0.5 percent of the funds in the individual accounts. In years when the reserves are less, 0.5 percent of the workers' contributions are deposited into the reserves.

The benefits in these funds are further insured through a central Guarantee Fund in which all pension funds must participate, at a required rate that varies between 0.3 and 0.5 percent of contributions to the pension funds. In addition, Hungarian law requires that the average annual value of the Guarantee Fund may not be less than 0.3 percent or more than 1.5 percent of the total combined assets of the funds it is insuring. The Hungarian government may order Hungarian pension funds to make special contributions to the Guarantee Fund if the assets of the fund are insufficient to meet its financial obligations. Moreover, it may borrow from the National Bank of Hungary, with the central budget of the government of Hungary guaranteeing repayment of the loan. If the assets of the Guarantee Fund exceed the upper limits allowed, it will suspend the required payment of contributions from pension funds.

Thus, the Guarantee Fund provides a backup if the pension fund cannot fulfill the minimum rate of return. It also guarantees the minimum benefit, providing the additional funds if the worker's account is insufficient.

Mandatory Individual Accounts without Guarantees

While most countries with mandatory individual accounts provide rate-of-return guarantees, some do not. In certain cases, the latter have regulations that limit the financial market risk that plans can take; alternatively, the plans may provide a small part of retirement income, being a second tier on top of basic social security. Latvia has established a second-tier mandatory defined contribution system without a rate-of-return guarantee. It has strict limits on the investments that pension funds can hold, which reduce the risk of these funds and form a partial substitute for a guarantee. Sweden has a mandatory second-tier defined contribution plan without a rate-of-return guarantee; however, the plan has a required contribution rate of only 2.5 percent, compared to one of 16 percent for the notional defined contribution plan that forms the first tier. Australia does not provide a minimum rate-of-return guarantee, but it offers a relatively generous means-tested benefit that serves as a form of benefit guarantee. If the contribution rate for the mandated individual accounts is comparatively low, and the program is a second tier on top of a relatively generous social security plan, a rate-of-return guarantee is typically not provided.

CONCLUSIONS

Perhaps the most important criticism of mandatory defined contribution systems, although one not accepted by all pension analysts, is that they may place too much financial market risk on workers. This view depends in part on the size of the plans and whether they are add-ons or carve-outs from traditional defined-benefit social security programs. Because of this concern, most mandatory defined contribution systems that provide the majority of retirement benefits offer benefit or rate-of-return guarantees. (See the discussion of guarantees and financial market risk in Chapter 1 of this book.)

Among countries that provide guarantees, these are typically backed by some type of reserve or insurance fund, often with the government providing further support if those sources should fail. In Switzerland, by contrast, the first source of backing is additional contributions by employers. The reserve funds are often financed through contributions from the pension fund in years when the rate of return exceeds a set level, but in some countries special contributions are made by employers or employees into the funds.

Many of the countries providing rate-of-return guarantees do so relative to a financial market index. These features limit the extent to which participants will receive different rates of return, which is an inherent aspect of allowing participants choice as to how their accounts are invested, but do not protect against capital market risk. Absolute rate-of-return guarantees, however, may provide protection against some degree of capital market fluctuations; the three-year decline in financial markets starting in the year 2000 proved that these types of guarantees can prove to be too expensive to maintain during a prolonged downturn.

Note

1. Pennacchi (1999) has analyzed the guarantees used in Uruguay and Chile, while Lindset (2001) analyzes guarantees more generically.

Appendix B

Labor Market Distortions Due to Contribution Evasion and Avoidance

Contribution evasion occurs when employees and employers do not make required social security payments. This situation is pandemic in the mandatory account systems in Latin America, with only 10 to 60 percent of the workers required to contribute actually doing so (Gill, Packard, and Yermo 2005). (See also the discussion in Chapter 7 of this book.) Even social security in the United States and other OECD countries has substantial underpayment due to workers' participation in the "underground" or "informal" economy (Gillion et al. 2000). While it is difficult for wage and salary earners to evade mandatory social security contributions, it is much easier for self-employed and contract workers, household employees, owners and employees of small businesses, and casual laborers.

Contribution evasion is a problem in both mandatory defined benefit and mandatory individual accounts. Such behavior occurs for several reasons with mandatory individual accounts (Bailey and Turner 2001). First, guaranteed minimum or means-tested benefits reduce the incentive for low-income workers to contribute if the outcome from their payments is not much larger than the guaranteed benefit. In Chile, for example, the provision of a guaranteed minimum benefit after 20 years of contributions may discourage low-wage earners from paying further. To avoid contributing, some workers may move into the informal sector.

Myopic workers prefer not to contribute toward their future retirement benefits and to keep their money for current consumption, regardless of the type of retirement income system. Myopic workers have a high rate of time discount, meaning that they place little weight on planning for future periods. This perspective is a reason why social security programs are mandatory (Gillion et al. 2000). Because myopic workers place little value on future benefits, they are more likely to view required contributions as a tax. As a tax, the contributions would have distortionary effects on their decisions relating to work.

Low-income workers, small firms, and people and businesses in financial distress are more likely to evade making social security contributions because they place higher priority on expenses with more immediate payoff, such as health benefits (Bailey and Turner 2001). Low-income workers may feel that the level of the mandatory contribution rate is too high and not contribute for that reason.

The efforts of employers and workers to evade social security contributions for mandatory individual accounts may affect labor market outcomes. Employers may hire some workers informally, paying them in cash, rather than as part of the official payroll. Doing so not only eliminates contributing to social security, it deprives workers of labor market protections of law. Similarly, employers may claim workers are contractors rather than employees, which would also have the dual effect of evading contributions and withholding labor protections provided to employees.

Contribution evasion for mandatory individual accounts may be easier in some jobs than in others and may affect one's choice of employment. People may work in the underground or informal economy in part to evade mandatory social security contributions and taxes.

Contribution avoidance is closely related. While contribution evasion is the illegal failure to make mandatory contributions, contribution avoidance occurs when workers and employers take legal steps so as not to be required to contribute. Contribution avoidance occurs when employers structure work and payment so that the people who work for them will not be classified as employees. It also occurs when firms structure compensation in order to reduce the part that is covered by social security. This can be done by small enterprise owners when they take compensation as profits rather than as wages.

Contribution evasion and avoidance may take place because of the effect of taxes and social security payments when collected together. Thus, social security contribution evasion often is an aspect of income tax evasion. It may distort labor market activity, which has resultant welfare costs.

Contribution evasion is only possible when the government fails to enforce mandatory contributions. In Chile, for example, it is the employers' responsibility to ensure that their workers contribute, but the government makes little effort to enforce the mandatory contribution law. Lax enforcement in other Latin American countries is evident from the low participation rates there as well (Gill, Packard, and Yermo 2005).

References

Agnew, Julie, Pierluigi Balduzzi, and Annika Sundén. 2000. "Portfolio Choice, Trading, and Returns in a Large 401(k) Plan." CRR Working Paper 2000-06. Boston: Center for Retirement Research, Boston College. http://ideas.repec.org/p/crr/crrwps/2000-06.htm (accessed October 14, 2005).

American Funds Capital Income Builder. 2003. *Seminannual Report for the Six Months Ending April 30*. Norfolk, VA: American Funds Capital Income Builder.

Ameriks, John. 2002. "Recent Trends in the Selection of Retirement Income Streams among TIAA-CREF Participants." *Research Dialogue* 74 (December): 1–19. http://www.tiaa-crefinstitute.org/research/dialogue/74.html (accessed October 14, 2005).

Ameriks, John, and Stephen P. Zeldes. 2004. "How Do Household Portfolio Shares Vary with Age?" TIAA-CREF Institute Working Paper 6-120101. http://www.ifk_cfs.de/papers/rtn0505_paper_Ameriks_Zeldes.pdf (accessed October 14, 2005).

Baer, Gregory, and Gary Gensler. 2002. *The Great Mutual Fund Trap: An Investment Recovery Plan. How Americans Are Losing Billions to the Mutual Fund and Brokerage Industries—and How You Can Earn More with Less Risk*. New York: Broadway Books.

Bailey, Clive, and John Turner. 2001. "Strategies to Reduce Contribution Evasion in Social Security Financing." *World Development* 29(2): 385–393.

Bajtelsmit, Vickie L., and Alexandra Bernasek. 1996. "Why Do Women Invest Differently than Men?" *Financial Counseling and Planning* 7(1996):1–10.

Bajtelsmit, Vickie L., and Nancy A. Jianakoplos. 2001. "Household Stock Investing: Inside versus Outside the Retirement Plan." *Benefits Quarterly* 17(2): 49–60.

Bajtelsmit, Vickie L., and Jack L. VanDerhei. 1996. "Risk Aversion and Pension Investment Choices." In *Positioning Pensions for the Twenty-First Century*, Michael S. Gordon, Olivia S. Mitchell, and Mark M. Twinney, eds. Philadelphia: University of Pennsylvania Press, pp. 45–66.

Barber, Brad, and Terrance Odean. 2001. "Boys Will Be Boys: Gender, Overconfidence, and Common Stock Investment." *Quarterly Journal of Economics* 116(February): 261–292.

Barr, Nicholas. 2001. *The Welfare State as Piggy Bank*. Oxford: Oxford University Press.

Bateman, Hazel. 2001. "Disclosure of Superannuation Fees and Charges." Discussion Paper 03/04, prepared for the Australian Institute of Superannuation Trustees. Sydney, Australia: Centre for Pensions and Superannuation.

Benartzi, Shlomo, and Richard S. Thaler. 2001. "Naïve Diversification Strategies in Defined Contribution Savings Plans." *American Economic Review* 91(1): 79–98.

Benefitnews.com. 2002. "401(k) Activity Spikes in July as Equities Get Beaten Down." *Connect Newsletter,* August 9. http://www.benefitnews.com (accessed December 21, 2005).

Betson, Fennell. 2001. "One in Five Swedes Makes Active PPM Choice." *Investments & Pensions Europe—IPE.com.* http://www.ipe.com/article. asp?article=11880 (accessed September 11, 2001).

Biggs, Andrew G. 2002. "Personal Accounts in a Down Market: How Recent Stock Market Declines Affect the Social Security Reform Debate." Briefing Paper No. 74. Washington, DC: Cato Institute.

Black, Fisher. 1980. "The Tax Consequences of Long Run Pension Policy." *Financial Analysts Journal* 36(5): 17–23.

Blake, David. 1995. *Pension Schemes and Pension Funds in the United Kingdom*. Oxford: Oxford University Press.

Blake, David, and John Board. 2000. "Measuring Value Added in the Pensions Industry." *Geneva Papers on Risk and Insurance* 25(4): 539–567.

Bodie, Zvi. 2001. "Retirement Investing: A New Approach." Pension Research Council Working Paper 2001-8. Philadelphia: Wharton School, University of Pennsylvania.

———. 2003. "An Analysis of Investment Advice to Retirement Plan Participants." In *The Pension Challenge: Risk Transfers and Retirement Income Security*, Olivia S. Mitchell and Kent Smetters, eds. Oxford: Oxford University Press, pp. 19–32.

Bolger, Andrew. 2001. "Warning over Lack of Advice on Low Cost Pensions." *Financial Times*, November 7, A:6.

Boyle, Phelim, and Mary Hardy. 2002. "Guaranteed Annuity Options." Paper presented at the 37th Actuarial Research Conference, Society of Actuaries, held in Waterloo, ON, Canada, August 7–10.

Brown, Jeffrey R. 1999. "Differential Mortality and the Value of Individual Account Retirement Annuities." NBER Working Paper No. 7560. Cambridge, MA: National Bureau of Economic Research.

Budd, Alan, and Nigel Campbell. 1998. "The Roles of the Public and Private Sectors in the U.K. Pension System." In *Privatizing Social Security*, Martin Feldstein, ed. Chicago: University of Chicago Press, pp. 99–133.

Burkhauser, Richard, and John Turner. 1985. "Is the Social Security Payroll Tax a Tax?" *Public Finance Quarterly* 13(3): 253–267.

Burtless, Gary. 2000a. "How Would Financial Risk Affect Retirement Income under Individual Accounts?" Issue Brief No. 5. Boston: Center for Retirement Research, Boston College.

————. 2000b. "Social Security Privatization and Financial Market Risk: Lessons from U.S. Financial History." Center on Social and Economic Dynamics Working Paper No. 10. Washington, DC: Brookings Institution.

Canadian Press. 2005. "Retirement Saving, Financial Planning More Stressful Than Seeing Dentist: RBC." *Canadian Press*, February 21. http://canada.com/finance/rrsp/archives.html (accessed October 12, 2005).

CB Capitales. 1999. *Comentario Macroeconómico: Primera Quincena de Abril de 1999*. Santiago, Chile: CB Capitales. http://www.cb.cl/newcbcl/estudios/macro_temas.asp?Codid=35&Temad=Rebaja%20de%20aranceles%20y%20el%20tema%20de%20las%20salvaguardias&Pos=0&opcEditorial ComMacro=C (accessed October 24, 2005).

Central Intelligence Agency (CIA). 2005. *CIA World Fact Book, 2005*. Washington, DC: CIA. http://www.cia.gov/cia/publications/factbook/ (accessed October 26, 2005).

Chlon, Agnieszka, Marek Góra, and Michal Rutkowski. 1999. "Shaping Pension Reform in Poland: Security through Diversity." Social Protection Discussion Paper No. 9923. Washington, DC: World Bank. http://wbln0018.worldbank.org/HDNet/hddocs.nsf/0/5224C316362AA621852567EF005611B6?C (accessed October 12, 2005).

Clark, Robert L., Gordon P. Goodfellow, Sylvester J. Schieber, and Drew Warwick. 1996. "Making the Most of 401(k) Plans: Who's Choosing What and Why?" In *Positioning Pensions for the Twenty-First Century*, Michael S. Gordon, Olivia S. Mitchell, and Mark M. Twinney, eds. Philadelphia: University of Pennsylvania Press, pp. 96–138.

Cogan, John F., and Olivia S. Mitchell. 2003. "Perspectives from the President's Commission on Social Security Reform." *Journal of Economic Perspectives* 17(2): 149–172.

Cohen, Norma. 2005. "A Bloody Mess: How Has Britain's Privatization Scheme Worked Out? Well, Today, They're Looking Enviably upon Social Security." *American Prospect* 16(2). http://prospect.org/web/page.ww?name=View+Author&section=root&id=1186 (accessed October 26, 2005).

Coronado, Julia Lynn. 1997. "Behavioral Responses to Social Security Privatization: Evidence from the Chilean Reform." PhD Dissertation, University of Texas–Austin.

Cutler, David. 1999. "Comment on H. Aaron, 'Social Security: Tune It Up, Don't Trade It In.'" In *Should the United States Privatize Social Security?* Henry Aaron and John Shoven, eds. Cambridge, MA: MIT Press, pp. 123–133.

Dailey, Lorna M., and John Turner. 1992. "U.S. Private Pensions in World Perspective, 1970–89." In *Trends in Pensions 1992*, John A. Turner and

Daniel J. Beller, eds. Washington, DC: U.S. Government Printing Office, pp. 11–34.

Diamond, Peter A. 1998. "The Economics of Social Security Reform." In *Framing the Social Security Debate: Values, Politics and Economics*, R. Douglas Arnold, Michael J. Graetz, and Alicia Munnell, eds. Washington, DC: Brookings Institution, pp. 38–64.

Diamond, Peter A., and Peter R. Orszag. 2004. *Saving Social Security: A Balanced Approach*. Washington, DC: Brookings Institution.

Disney, Richard, Robert Palacios, and Edward Whitehouse. 1999. "Individual Choice of Pension Arrangement as a Pension Reform Strategy." IFS Working Paper Series, No. W99/18. London: Institute for Fiscal Studies.

Economic Systems Inc. 1998. *Study of 401(k) Plan Fees and Expenses*. Report to the U.S. Department of Labor, Pension and Welfare Benefits Administration. Washington, DC: USDOL.

Edwards, Sebastian. 1998. "The Chilean Reform: A Pioneering Program." In *Privatizing Social Security*, Martin Feldstein, ed. Chicago: University of Chicago Press, pp. 33–57.

Elder, Harold W. 1999. "Who Makes Major Financial Decisions in the Households of Older Americans?" Presented at the Academy of Financial Services meeting, held in Orlando, FL, October.

Ellsberg, Daniel. 1961. "Risk, Ambiguity, and the Savage Axioms." *Quarterly Journal of Economics* 75(4): 643–669.

Engström, Stefan, and Anna Westerberg. 2003. "Reversed Default Behavior in a New Defined Contribution Pension System." SSE/EFI Working Paper Series in Economics and Finance No. 527. Stockholm, Sweden: Stockholm School of Economics.

Feldstein, Martin, Elena Ranguelova, and Andrew Samwick. 1999. "The Transition to Investment-Based Social Security When Portfolio Returns and Capital Profitability Are Uncertain." NBER Working Paper No. 7016. Cambridge, MA: National Bureau of Economic Research.

Ferguson, Karen, and Kate Blackwell. 1995. *Pensions in Crisis: Why the System Is Failing America and How You Can Protect Your Future*. New York: Arcade Publishing.

Fox, Louise, and Edward Palmer. 2001. "New Approaches to Multipillar Pension Systems: What in the World Is Going On?" In *New Ideas about Old Age Security: Toward Sustainable Pension Systems in the 21st Century*, Robert Holzmann and Joseph E. Stiglitz, eds. Washington, DC: World Bank, pp. 90–132.

Friedberg, Leora, and Anthony Webb. 2000. "The Impact of 401(k) Plans on Retirement." Discussion Paper No. 2000-30. San Diego: University of California, San Diego.

Gale, William, and James Scholz. 1994. "IRAs and Household Saving." *American Economic Review* 84(5): 1233–1260.

Gill, Indermit S., Truman Packard, and Juan Yermo. 2005. *Keeping the Promise of Social Security in Latin America.* Washington, DC: World Bank.

Gillion, Colin, John Turner, Clive Bailey, and Denis Latulippe, eds. 2000. *Social Security Pensions: Development and Reform.* Geneva: International Labor Office.

Grushka, Carlos. 2001. "Administrative Costs, Investment Performance and Transparency: A View from Latin America." In *Private Pension Systems: Administrative Costs and Reforms.* Paris: Organisation for Economic Cooperation and Development (OECD), pp. 175–182.

Gustman, Alan L., and Thomas L. Steinmeier. 1998. "Privatizing Social Security: First-Round Effects of a Generic, Voluntary, Privatized U.S. Social Security System." In *Privatizing Social Security*, Martin Feldstein, ed. Chicago: University of Chicago Press, pp. 313–357.

———. 2005. "Retirement Effects of Proposals by the President's Commission to Strengthen Social Security." *National Tax Journal* 58(1): 27–49.

Habitat. 1991. *Diez Años de Historia del Sistema de AFP.* Santiago, Chile: Habitat.

Harrysson, Lars, and Michael O'Brien. 2003. "Pension Reform in New Zealand: A Comparative Analysis of Path Dependent Reform Processes." Paper presented at the 4th International Research Conference on Social Security, held in Antwerp, Belgium, May 5–7.

Hart, Lawrence E., Mark Kearney, Carol Musil, and Kelly Olsen. 2001. *SSA's Estimates of Administrative Costs under a Centralized Program of Individual Accounts.* Washington, DC: Social Security Administration. http://www.ssa.gov/policy/docs/research/rr2000-01rev.pdf (accessed October 20, 2005).

Herbertsson, Tryggvi Thor, J. Michael Orszag, and Peter R. Orszag. 2000. *Retirement in the Nordic Countries: Prospects and Proposals for Reform.* A Report prepared for the Nordic Council of Ministers, Copenhagen, May 10.

Hermes, Sharon, and Teresa Ghilarducci. Forthcoming. "How 401(k)s Destabilize the Macro-Economy and Affect Women's and Men's Retirement Decisions." In *Work Options for Mature Americans*, Teresa Ghilarducci and John Turner, eds. Notre Dame, IN: University of Notre Dame Press.

Hewitt Associates. 2002. "Switzerland: New BVG Minimum Interest Rate Affects All Pension Plans." Special Report. http://was4.hewitt.com/hewitt/resource/legislative_updates/europe/eufocusspec_dec02.htm (accessed October 13, 2005).

Hinz, Richard, David McCarthy, and John Turner. 1996. "Are Women Conservative Investors? Gender Differences in Participant-Directed Pension Investments." In *Positioning Pensions for the Twenty-First Century*, Michael S. Gordon, Olivia S. Mitchell, and Mark M. Twinney, eds. Philadelphia: University of Pennsylvania Press, pp. 91–103.

Hinz, Richard P., and John Turner. 1998. "Pension Coverage Initiatives: Why Don't Workers Participate?" In *Living with Defined Contribution Pensions*, Olivia S. Mitchell and Sylvester J. Schieber, eds. Philadelphia: University of Pennsylvania Press, pp. 17–37.

Holden, Sarah, and Jack VanDerhei. 2001. "401(k) Asset Allocation, Account Balances, and Loan Activity in 2000." EBRI Issue Brief No. 239. Washington, DC: Employee Benefit Research Institute.

Hungary, Republic of. 1997. *Act LXXXII of 1997 on Private Pensions and Private Pension Funds.* http://siteresources.worldbank.org/INTPENSIONS/Resources/395443-1122047906143/PenLegHungary1997.pdf (accessed October 13, 2005).

Huss, R. Bradford. 2003. "Allocation of Expenses in Defined Contribution Plans." *Benefits Report* 12(6): 1–3. http://truckerhuss.com/pub/v12n6news.pdf (accessed June 2003).

International Social Security Administration (ISSA). 2003. *Complementary & Private Pensions throughout the World, 2003.* Geneva: ISSA. http://www.issa.int/pdf/publ/summary/CPP.htm (accessed October 13, 2005).

Iyengar, Sheena S., Wei Jiang, and Gur Huberman. 2004. "How Much Choice Is Too Much? Determinants of Individual Contributions in 401(k) Retirement Plans." In *Pension Design and Structure: New Lessons from Behavioral Finance*, Olivia S. Mitchell and Stephen P. Utkus, eds. Oxford: Oxford University Press, pp. 83–97.

James, Estelle. 2005. "How It's Done in Chile: Personal Accounts—with Strings Attached." *Washington Post*, February 13, B:2. http://www.washingtonpost.com/wp-dyn/articles/A18478-2005Feb12.html (accessed February 15, 2005).

James, Estelle, Alejandra Cox Edwards, and Rebecca Wong. 2003. "The Gender Impact of Social Security Reform." *Journal of Pension Economics and Finance* 2(2): 181–219.

James, Estelle, Guillermo Martinez, and Augusto Iglesias. 2004. "The Payout Stage in Chile: Who Annuitizes and Why?" Unpublished paper. http://www.estellejames.com/downloads/payout-chile.pdf (accessed December 21, 2005).

James, Estelle, James Smalhout, and Dmitri Vittas. 2002. "Administrative Costs and the Organization of Individual Account Systems: A Comparative Perspective." In *Private Pension Systems: Administrative Costs and*

Reforms. Paris: Organisation for Economic Co-operation and Development (OECD), pp. 17–83.

Jarvenpaa, Perttu. 2001. "Non-Switching Swedes Prompt PPM Call Centre Sale." *Investment & Pensions Europe (IPE) Newsline.* http://www.ipe-newsline.com/article.asp?article=11129 (accessed March 30, 2001).

Jefferson, Regina T. 2000. "Rethinking the Risk of Defined Contribution Plans." *Tax Notes* 88(August 28): 1171–1172.

Jianakoplos, Nancy Ammon. 1999. "Invest as I Say, Not as I Do? Gender Differences in Financial Risk Preferences." Paper presented to the 74th Annual Western Economic International Conference, held in San Diego, CA, July 6–10.

Jianakoplos, Nancy Ammon, and Alexandra Bernasek. 1998. "Are Women More Risk Averse?" *Economic Inquiry* 36(4): 620–630.

Jossi, Frank. 2003. "Mutual Fund Firms Support 401(k) Fee Disclosure Efforts." *St. Louis Business Journal.* http://www.bizjournals.com/stlouis/1998/03/23/focus13.html (accessed March 23, 2003).

Kehl, David. 2002. "Superannuation Preservation Rules: A Summary." *Research Notes* No. 22. Canberra, Australia: Information and Research Services, Department of the Parliamentary Library.

Kingston, Geoffrey H. 2000. "Efficient Timing of Retirement." *Review of Economic Dynamics* 3(4): 831–840.

Korczyk, Sophie, and John Turner. 2003. "Transparency in Defined Contribution Plans." Unpublished manuscript. Washington, DC: AARP.

Kotlikoff, Laurence J., Kent A. Smetters, and Jan Walliser. 1998. "Opting Out of Social Security and Adverse Selection." NBER Working Paper No. 6430. Cambridge, MA: National Bureau of Economic Research.

Kritzer, Barbara. 2000. "Social Security Privatization in Latin America." *Social Security Bulletin* 63(2): 17–23.

Lachance, Marie-Eve, and Olivia S. Mitchell. 2003. "Understanding Individual Account Guarantees." In *The Pension Challenge: Risk Transfers and Retirement Income Security,* Olivia S. Mitchell and Kent Smetters, eds. Oxford: Oxford University Press, pp. 159–186.

Lerner, Max. 1957. *America as a Civilization.* Vol.1, *The Basic Frame.* New York: Simon and Schuster.

Lillard, Lee A., and Robert J. Willis. 2001. "Cognition and Wealth: The Importance of Probabilistic Thinking." Working Paper No. 2001-07. Ann Arbor, MI: University of Michigan Retirement Research Center.

Lindset, Snorre. 2001. "Defined Contribution and Defined Benefit Pension Plans with Guarantees." Unpublished paper. Bergen, Norway: Norwegian School of Economics and Business Administration.

Lucas, Lori. 2000. "Under the Microscope: A Closer Look at the Diversification and Risk Taking Behavior of 401(k) Participants and How Plan Sponsors Can Address Key Investing Issues." *Benefits Quarterly* 16(4): 24–30.

Mackenzie, G.A. 2002. "The Role of Private Sector Annuities Markets in an Individual Accounts Reform of a Public Pension Plan." Working Paper No. 02/161. Washington, DC: International Monetary Fund.

Madrian, Brigitte C., and Dennis F. Shea. 2001. "The Power of Suggestion: Inertia in 401(k) Participation and Savings Behavior." *Quarterly Journal of Economics* 116(4): 1149–1187.

Mahoney, Paul G. 2004. "Manager-Investor Conflicts in Mutual Funds." *Journal of Economic Perspectives* 18(2): 161–182.

Maurer, Raimond, and Christian Schlag. 2003. "Money-Back Guarantees in Individual Pension Accounts: Evidence from the German Pension Reform." Working Paper No. 2002/03. Frankfurt am Main, Germany: Center for Financial Studies.

McCarthy, David D., and John A. Turner. 1993. "Risk Classification and Sex Discrimination in Pension Plans." *Journal of Risk and Insurance* 60(1): 85–104.

———. 2000. "Pension Education: Does It Help? Does It Matter?" *Benefits Quarterly* 16(1): 64–72.

Mesa-Lago, Carmelo. 1997. "Comparative Analysis of the Structural Pension Reform in Eight Latin American Countries: Description, Evaluation and Lessons." In *Capitalization: The Bolivian Model of Social and Economic Reform*, Margaret H. Pierce, ed. Unpublished manuscript based on a joint collaboration of the Woodrow Wilson Center and the North-South Center. Washington, DC: Woodrow Wilson Center.

Mitchell, Olivia S., and John Piggott. 2000. "Developments in Retirement Provision: Global Trends and Lessons from Australia and the U.S." Pension Research Council Working Paper No. 2000-2. Philadelphia: Wharton School, University of Pennsylvania.

Money Marketing. 2004. "Pru and NU Tell Policyholders to Go Back to S2P." *Money Marketing,* November 25.

Mosconi, Gustavo Márquez. 1997. "An Assessment of Pension System Reform in Uruguay in 1995." Paper prepared for the Social Programs Division, Social Programs and Sustainable Development Department, Inter-American Development Bank. Washington, DC: Inter-American Development Bank.

Muller, Leslie. 2000. "Investment Choice in Defined Contribution Plans: The Effects of Retirement Education on Asset Allocation." Unpublished paper. Washington, DC: Social Security Administration.

Munnell, Alicia H., Kevin E. Cahill, and Natalia A. Jivan. 2003. "How Has the Shift to 401(k)s Affected the Retirement Age?" Issue Brief No. 13. Boston: Center for Retirement Research, Boston College.

Munnell, Alicia H., Annika Sundén, and Catherine Taylor. 2000. "What Determines 401(k) Participation and Contributions?" Working Paper No. 2000-12. Boston: Center for Retirement Research, Boston College.

Murthi, Manta, J. Michael Orszag, and Peter R. Orszag. 2001. "Administrative Costs under a Decentralized Approach to Individual Accounts: Lessons from the United Kingdom." In *New Ideas about Old Age Security*, Robert Holtzmann and Joseph E. Stiglitz, eds. Washington, DC: World Bank, pp. 308–335.

National Academy of Social Insurance (NASI). 2005. *Uncharted Waters: Paying Benefits from Individual Accounts in Federal Retirement Policy*. Washington, DC: NASI.

New, Bill. 1999. "Paternalism and Public Policy." *Economics and Philosophy* 15(1): 63–83.

Norris, Floyd. 2003. "Mutual Funds, Calls for Reform." *New York Times*, June 15. http://www.nytimes.com/2003/06/15/business/yourmoney/15MUTU. html?th (accessed June 15, 2003).

Nyce, Steven A., and Sylvester J. Schieber. 2005. *The Economic Implications of Aging Societies: The Costs of Living Happily Ever After*. Cambridge: Cambridge University Press.

Organisation for Economic Co-operation and Development (OECD). 1998. "The Chilean Pension System." Working Paper AWP 5.6. Paris: OECD.

Orszag, Peter R., and Robert Greenstein. 2001. *Voluntary Individual Accounts for Social Security: What Are the Costs?* Washington, DC: Center on Budget and Policy Priorities. http://www.cbpp.org/8-21-01socsec.htm (accessed October 13, 2005).

Palmer, Edward. 2000. "The Swedish Pension Reform Model: Framework and Issues." SP Discussion Paper No. 0012. Washington, DC: World Bank.

———. 2001. "Sweden's New Pension System." Statement before the Subcommittee on Social Security of the House Committee on Ways and Means. Hearing on Social Security and Pension Reform: Lessons from Other Countries, Washington, DC, July 31.

Pennacchi, George G. 1999. "The Value of Guarantees on Pension Fund Returns." *Journal of Risk and Insurance* 66(2): 219–237.

Pensions Commission. 2005. *A New Pension Settlement for the Twenty-First Century: The Second Report of the Pensions Commission*. London: Pensions Commission.

Pensions Policy Institute. 2003. *State Pension Models*. London: Pensions Policy Institute.

Piñera, José. 2001. "Toward a World of Worker-Capitalists." Paper presented at the Cato Institute conference "Privatizing Social Security: Beyond the Theory," held in Washington, DC, February 6.

———. 2003. "Free Trade and Social Security Choice." Daily commentary. Washington, DC: Cato Institute, June 15. http:www.cato.org/dailys/06-15-03.html (accessed June 20, 2003).

Pollan, Stephen M., and Mark Levine. 2001. "Money Forever: Break All the Rules—Invest as if You're Going to Live to 100." *Modern Maturity* 44R(2): 73–88.

Poterba, James M. 2001. "Taxation and Portfolio Structure: Issues and Implications." NBER Working Paper No. 8223. Cambridge, MA: National Bureau of Economic Research. http://www.nber.org/papers/w8223 (accessed May 17, 2003).

Premium Pension Authority (PPM). 2001. "Information and News on Your Premium Pension." *PPM Nyheter* 2001(3). http://www.ppm.nu/dbfiles/pdf/377.pdf (accessed October 13, 2005).

———. 2002. "Award in the Arbitration Proceedings between CSC and PPM." Press release, October 3. http://www.ppm.nu/dbfiles/pdf/824.pdf (accessed May 20, 2003).

———. 2003. "Your Whole Life Counts." http://www.forsakringskassan.se/pension/hjalp/docs/RFV_Dap_ENG.pdf (accessed October 13, 2005).

President's Commission to Strengthen Social Security. 2001. *Strengthening Social Security and Creating Personal Wealth for All Americans: Report of the President's Commission.* Washington, DC: President's Commission to Strengthen Social Security.

Quinn, Jane Bryant. 2002. "Burned! Why We Need to Fix the 401(k)." *Newsweek,* August 19, pp. 25–31.

Reagan, Patricia, and John Turner. 1997. "Measuring the Sensitivity of Pension Coverage Rates to Changes in Marginal Tax Rates." *Proceedings of the 89th Annual Conference on Taxation.* Washington, DC: National Tax Association, pp. 112–115.

———. 2000. "Did the Decline in Marginal Tax Rates during the 1980s Reduce Pension Coverage?" In *Employee Benefits and Labor Markets in Canada and the United States,* William T. Alpert and Stephen A. Woodbury, eds. Kalamazoo, MI: W.E. Upjohn Institute for Employment Research, pp. 475–497.

Reid, Dickon. 2002. "PPM Mis-Sells Shares for 11,000 Members." *Investment & Pensions Europe (IPE) Newsline,* January 7. http://www.ipe-newsline.com/article.asp?article=12370 (accessed January 7, 2002).

Rein, Martin, and John Turner. 2001. "Public-Private Interactions: Mandatory Pensions in Australia, the Netherlands and Switzerland." *Review of Population and Social Policy* 10(2001): 107–153.

———. 2004. "Pathways to Pension Coverage." In *Reforming Pensions in Europe: Evolution of Pension Financing and Sources of Retirement Income,*

Gerard Hughes and James Stewart, eds. Cheltenham, UK: Edward Elgar, pp. 285–300.

Rodriguez, Jacobo L. 1999. *Chile's Private Pension System at 18: Its Current State and Future Challenges.* The Cato Project on Social Security Privatization, No. 17. Washington, DC: Cato Institute.

———. 2001. "The Current State of Chile's Private Pension System." Statement before the Subcommittee on Social Security of the House Committee on Ways and Means. Hearing on Social Security and Pension Reform: Lessons from Other Countries. http://www.cato.org/testimony/ct-jr073101 .html (accessed November 10, 2001).

Rosenblatt, Robert A. 2001. "Hurdles Big, Small for Retirement Reform." *Los Angeles Times,* June 13. http://www.latimes.com/print/asection/20010613/ t000049187.html (accessed June 13, 2001).

Samuelson, William, and Richard J. Zeckhauser. 1988. "Status Quo Bias in Decision Making." *Journal of Risk and Uncertainty* 1(1): 7–59.

Sandul, Irina. 2002. "Private Funds Tackling Growing Pension Woes." New York: Global Action on Aging. http://www.globalaging.org/pension/world/ privateR.htm (accessed April 12, 2002).

Schieber, Sylvester J., and John B. Shoven. 1999. *The Real Deal: The History and Future of Social Security.* New Haven, CT: Yale University Press.

Seligman, Jason S., and Jeffrey B. Wenger. 2005. "Asynchronous Risk: Unemployment, Equity Markets, and Retirement Savings." Upjohn Institute Working Paper 05-114. Kalamazoo, MI: W.E. Upjohn Institute for Employment Research. http://www.upjohninstitute.org/publications/wp/05-114.pdf (accessed November 1, 2005).

Shoven, John B. 1999. "The Location and Allocation of Assets in Pension and Conventional Savings Accounts." NBER Working Paper No. 7007. Cambridge, MA: National Bureau of Economic Research. http://www.nber.org/ papers/w7007 (accessed February 20, 2000).

Sinha, Tapen. 1999. "Some Surprising Results of the AFOREs in Mexico." *Benefits & Compensation International* 29(5): 23.

Sjunde AP-fonden (Seventh AP Fund). 2003a. *Annual Report 2002, Part 1.* http://www.ap7.se/pdf/Annual_report_2002_1.pdf (accessed October 13, 2005).

———. 2003b. *Annual Report 2002, Part 2.* http://www.ap7.se/pdf/Annual_ report_2002_2.pdf (accessed October 13, 2005).

Social Security Administration (SSA). 1999. *Social Security Programs throughout the World.* SSA Publication No. 13-11805. Washington, DC: Social Security Administration.

Superintendente de Administradoras de Fondos de Pensiones (SAFP). 2001.

"Información Estadistica y Financiera." Santiago, Chile: SAFP. http://www
.safp.cl/inf_estadistica/index.html (accessed October 13, 2005).

Takayama, Noriyuki. 2005. "Pension Issues in Japan." Seminar presentation at AARP offices, Washington, DC, September 12.

Thaler, Richard H. 2005. "Libertarian Paternalism, Behavioral Economics, and Public Policy." Inaugural lecture, AARP Public Policy Institute's Twentieth Anniversary Invitational Lecture Series, Washington, DC, July 25.

Turner, John. 1984. "Population Age Structure and the Size of Social Security." *Southern Economic Journal* 50(April): 1131–1146.

————. 2000. "Mandatory Defined Contribution Pensions: Progress or Regression?" *International Social Security Review* 53(4): 25–36.

————. 2003. "Errors Workers Make in Managing 401(k) Investments." *Benefits Quarterly* (Winter): 75–82.

————. 2004. "Individual Accounts: Lessons from Sweden." *Ohio State Law Journal* 65(1): 27–44.

Turner, John, and Roy Guenther. 2005. "A Comparison of Early Retirement Pensions in the United States and Russia: The Pensions of Musicians." *Journal of Aging & Social Policy* 17(4): 61–74.

Turner, John, and David M. Rajnes. 1995. "'Pay or Play' Pensions in Japan and the United Kingdom." In *Social Security: Time for a Change*, Kevin Stephenson, ed. Greenwich, CT: JAI Press, pp. 87–103.

————. 1998. "Privatization of Retirement Income." In *The State of Social Welfare, 1997*, Peter Flora, Philip R. De Jong, Julian Le Grand, and Jun-Young Kim, eds. Aldershot, UK: Ashgate Publishing Ltd., pp. 283–296.

————. 2001. "Rate of Return Guarantees in Mandatory Defined Contribution Plans." *International Social Security Review* 54(4): 49–67.

————. 2003. "Rate of Return Guarantees in Voluntary Defined Contribution Plans." In *Risk Transfers and Retirement Income Security*, Olivia S. Mitchell and Kent Smetters, eds. Philadelphia: University of Pennsylvania Press, pp. 251–267.

————. 2004. "Defined Contribution Return and Annuity Guarantees in a Down Market." Unpublished paper. Washington, DC: AARP.

Turner, John, and Noriyasu Watanabe. 1995. *Private Pension Policies in Industrialized Countries*. Kalamazoo, MI: W.E. Upjohn Institute for Employment Research.

U.S. Department of Labor (USDOL). 2005. *Private Pension Plan Bulletin: Abstract of 2000 Form 5500 Annual Reports*. Washington, DC: U.S. Department of Labor, Employee Benefits Security Administration. http://www
.dol.gov/ebsa/PDF/2000pensionplanbulletin.pdf (accessed September 12, 2005).

U.S. Government Accounting Office (USGAO). 2003. "Mutual Funds: Greater

Transparency Needed in Disclosures to Investors." GAO-03-763. Washington, DC: General Accounting Office.

Valdés-Prieto, Salvador. 1994. "Administrative Charges in Pensions in Chile, Malaysia, Zambia, and the United States." Policy Research Working Paper No. 1372. Washington, DC: World Bank.

Vittas, Dmitri, and Augusto Iglesias. 1991. "The Rationale and Performance of Personal Pension Plans in Chile." World Bank Policy Research Working Paper No. 867. Washington, DC: World Bank.

Weaver, Kent. 2002. "Reforming Social Security: Lessons from Abroad." Paper presented at "Directions for Social Security Reform," the fourth annual conference of the Retirement Research Consortium, held in Washington, DC, May 30–31. http://www.bc.edu/centers/crr/papers/Fourth/cp_02_5_ weaver.pdf (accessed September 15, 2002).

Weisbenner, Scott. 1999. "Do Pension Plans with Participant Investment Choice Teach Households to Hold More Equity?" Finance and Economics Discussion Series Paper No. 1999-61. Washington, DC: Federal Reserve Board.

Whitehouse, Edward. 1998. "Pension Reform in Britain." Social Protection Discussion Paper No. 9810. Washington, DC: World Bank.

———. 2000. "Guarantees: Cost and Repercussions of Guaranteeing Funded Pension Benefits." *AXIA Viewpoint.* http://www.axiaecon.com (accessed January 18, 2000).

———. 2001. "Administrative Charges for Funded Pensions: Comparison and Assessment of 13 Countries." In *Private Pension Systems: Administrative Costs and Reforms.* Paris: OECD.

Williamson, John B. 2005. "A Quarter Century after Reform: An Update on Recent Social Security Developments in Chile." Policy Live: Conversations with the Experts. "Reforming Social Security: Lessons from Abroad," a symposium sponsored by the AARP Public Policy Institute, Washington, D.C., May 16.

World Bank. 1994. *Averting the Old Age Crisis.* New York: Oxford University Press.

———. 2000. "Annuities: Regulating Withdrawals from Individual Pension Accounts." *Pension Reform Primer*, February 25. http://www.aph.gov.au/ Senate/committee/superannuation_ctte/completed_inquiries/2002-04/ retirement/report/app08.pdf (accessed October 26, 2005).

The Author

John Turner is a senior policy advisor at the AARP Public Policy Institute in Washington, D.C. Previously, he worked at the International Labor Office in Geneva, Switzerland, where he coedited the book *Social Security Pensions: Development and Reform*. He has also worked in research offices at the U.S. Social Security Administration and at the U.S. Department of Labor, where he was the deputy director of the pension research office for nine years. He taught as an adjunct lecturer in economics at George Washington University and was a Fulbright scholar in France at the Institut de Recherches Economiques et Sociales. He is a member of the National Academy of Social Insurance, serves on the board of directors for the European Network for Research on Supplementary Pensions, and is chair of the pension committee on the Board of Pension and Health Benefits for the Baltimore-Washington conference of the United Methodist Church.

Turner has published more than 100 articles on pension and social security policy in the United States and other countries, among them Japan, Chile, the United Kingdom, Canada, Sweden, Indonesia, the Netherlands, Australia, and Russia. His articles have been translated into seven languages, including more than a dozen translated into Japanese. Along with coauthor David McCarthy, he received the annual award of the American Risk and Insurance Association in 1994 for the best article of the year in the *Journal of Risk and Insurance*. He has authored or edited ten books, two of which have been translated into Japanese and one of which is required reading for an examination of the American Society of Actuaries. Turner holds a PhD in economics from the University of Chicago.

Index

The italic letters *b, n,* and *t* following a page number indicate that the subject information of the heading is within a box, note, or table, respectively, on that page.

About the Institute

The W.E. Upjohn Institute for Employment Research is a nonprofit research organization devoted to finding and promoting solutions to employment-related problems at the national, state, and local levels. It is an activity of the W.E. Upjohn Unemployment Trustee Corporation, which was established in 1932 to administer a fund set aside by Dr. W.E. Upjohn, founder of The Upjohn Company, to seek ways to counteract the loss of employment income during economic downturns.

The Institute is funded largely by income from the W.E. Upjohn Unemployment Trust, supplemented by outside grants, contracts, and sales of publications. Activities of the Institute comprise the following elements: 1) a research program conducted by a resident staff of professional social scientists; 2) a competitive grant program, which expands and complements the internal research program by providing financial support to researchers outside the Institute; 3) a publications program, which provides the major vehicle for disseminating the research of staff and grantees, as well as other selected works in the field; and 4) an Employment Management Services division, which manages most of the publicly funded employment and training programs in the local area.

The broad objectives of the Institute's research, grant, and publication programs are to 1) promote scholarship and experimentation on issues of public and private employment and unemployment policy, and 2) make knowledge and scholarship relevant and useful to policymakers in their pursuit of solutions to employment and unemployment problems.

Current areas of concentration for these programs include causes, consequences, and measures to alleviate unemployment; social insurance and income maintenance programs; compensation; workforce quality; work arrangements; family labor issues; labor-management relations; and regional economic development and local labor markets.